6944

COMPETITIVENESS
HELPING
BUSINESS
TO WIN

Presented to Parliament by the President of the Board of Trade, and the Chancellor of the Exchequer, the Secretaries of State for Transport, Environment and Employment, the Chancellor of the Duchy of Lancaster, and the Secretaries of State for Scotland, Northern Ireland, Education and Wales by Command of Her Majesty May 1994

Cm 2563   LONDON: HMSO   £15.40 net

INTRODUCTION BY THE PRIME MINISTER

I have many ambitions for our country. I want to see higher living standards for our families, better schools and hospitals, strong defence, a cleaner environment, and a thriving artistic and cultural national life. All these depend on the success of the private wealth creating sector. To obtain a better quality of life for all, and to keep taxes as low as possible, we need our businesses to succeed.

Today, our companies face the most competitive environment they have ever seen. Change is relentless and swift. The global financial market never sleeps. Technology has shrunk the world. Free trade has opened new markets but it has also created new competitors. We cannot ignore these changes. To do so means certain decline.

We seek success from good foundations. We now have better industrial relations than ever before and our productivity is at an all time high. Inflation and interest rates are at historically low levels. But to make the most of these advantages we must continually improve our standards.

I am determined to set the framework for long-term success. We must prepare this country for the changing and challenging world of the next century. My aim is to create a climate in which our companies can beat the best. That is what this White Paper is all about.

Our first duty is to continue to win the battle against inflation. Low inflation has brought lower interest rates. It creates its own dynamic for investment and growth.

Second, I believe we must give our young people the highest standards of education and training. Their skills will be the key to our future. Education and training have undergone great but necessary change. This White Paper contains important new proposals to expand opportunity and to raise standards still higher.

Our aim is commercial and industrial success and the rewards it will bring for all of us. To achieve this we seek a new partnership between Government and industry – a partnership for prosperity in a competitive world.

John Major

Contents

SETTING THE SCENE

1.1 The UK faces a world of increasing change; of ever fiercer global competition; of growing consumer power; and a world in which our wealth is more and more dependent on the knowledge, skills and motivation of our people. These changes present both opportunities and challenges.

1.2 To prosper in this rapidly changing world, we have to improve our economic performance across the board. We must raise our productivity and adapt our skills, the way we work, and our products to new circumstances and opportunities.

The economic landscape is changing before our eyes...

1.3 The economies of the OECD now produce around half of world output as low income countries have exploited their potential for catching up the world leaders. Of the non-OECD countries, the Asian "Tigers" of Taiwan, Korea, Singapore and Hong Kong have grown at nearly 10 per cent a year for over 30 years. Hong Kong and Singapore now have average incomes which match those of the UK. Other countries in the Pacific Rim and beyond are also growing rapidly. Since 1980 India and Pakistan have grown at over 5 per cent, and China by over 9 per cent, a year. On some measures, the Chinese economy is now bigger than that of Japan.

1.4 In this new landscape, there is enormous new potential for growth. It has been greatly increased by the fall of communism. The population of Eastern Europe and the former Soviet Union exceeds that of the present European Community (EC). Educational standards are high, yet income levels are generally much lower. Successful stabilisation and economic reform programmes have transformed the outlook for many South American economies.

... as barriers to the movement of goods and capital fall...

1.5 Since the war international trade has been one of the main forces behind faster growth. As trade barriers have fallen trade has grown far more quickly than output. Since 1960, the volume of OECD trade has increased sevenfold, while output has only trebled.

1.6 Exports now account for around 20 per cent of GDP in the OECD countries. Although the majority of trade is in goods, services are taking a rising share. Trade with the dynamic Asian economies is small but growing fast. The pattern of trade with these economies is changing as they have increased their market shares in knowledge intensive sectors such as office equipment and telecommunications.

1.7 The recent GATT agreement will further reduce barriers to trade in goods and services. It will boost world trade by at least 12 per cent over the next decade or so, adding about $270 billion a year to world incomes. Within Europe, the creation of the

Single Market and its extension this year to the European Economic Area have created a market of 370 million consumers free of barriers to investment and trade.

1.8 During the 1980s international direct investment flows in the OECD grew over twice as quickly as did trade. Technology is being transferred ever more rapidly to where returns are the greatest. The ability of a nation to attract mobile capital depends increasingly on the skills and motivation of its workforce.

1.9 These changes will significantly increase average living standards throughout the world. They will present enormous opportunities and new markets for UK firms provided that we can supply the goods and services that others want to buy. For example, it has been estimated that by 2020 there will be more cars in countries outside the OECD than within it.

1.10 But the changes will also increase the pressure of competition. The rapid spread of capitalism, the opening of closed economies and the removal of rigid systems of central planning could bring a low cost labour force of 1.2 billion people on to world markets as producers as well as consumers.

... advances in technology open new markets and transform existing industries...

1.11 Advances in technology have always been one of the most important drivers of economic growth. The rate of innovation is increasing, making it both more difficult and more important that we keep in the forefront. As a leading Japanese businessman remarked: "if we do not make our own products obsolete, someone else will".

1.12 Technological change brings more sophisticated goods and services. Over the last two decades, world trade in high technology products has grown 50 per cent faster than overall trade. Information technology is creating new, high value markets around the world: for example, new markets are emerging for films, publishing, home services, multimedia entertainment and real time information. The value of software products in the US TV and video market was recently put at five times that of the hardware.

1.13 Industries increasingly rely on technology to achieve competitive advantage. The use of bar code technology has not only enabled retailers to respond more quickly to changes in customer demand but has also allowed better and faster baggage handling at airports.

1.14 Dramatic reductions in the cost of information are causing a radical and welcome shift of power from producers to consumers. Industry after industry has had to become more responsive to customers. More and more companies are planning a global supply infrastructure but thinking locally to provide what the customer wants.

... and population structures change.

1.15 The coming decades will see significant demographic changes. The population of the developing countries will continue to increase rapidly, as will the number of people aged 65 and over in the developed world. By 2030, it is expected that there will be fewer than three people of working age for each person over 65 in the West European members of the OECD, compared with five now. North America and Japan will be affected in the same way. Growth in the over 65 population in the UK will be slower than in many of our European partners.

1.16 The position of women is also changing. More young women are taking up paid work and more mothers are working after having children. In 1973 fewer than half the women of working age in the OECD were members of the labour force. By 1991 that figure had risen to over 60 per cent.

1.17 These changes will have significant effects on companies. They will no longer be able to count on a large flow of young people, but will be able to recruit from a larger pool of women. Firms will have to adjust to changes in demand for their products or services as the population ages, and as spending patterns evolve to reflect the changing role of women.

We cannot hide from change.

1.18 Developments in technology, communications and world trade mean that for manufacturing, and for a growing range of services, firms increasingly look all over the world for their suppliers. A major UK company now handles US customer reservations here and carries out data processing work in India. A UK publisher prepares text in India and prints in China. Even the smallest local company is operating in a global market – whether consciously or not – either directly, or as a supplier to a larger company.

1.19 Many of the drivers of change are beyond the control of governments. In the increasingly global market there is no hiding place, no comfortable backwater. Change will not stop and others will not rest. They will strive to pass us by. We must continually improve our performance.

Competitiveness is the key to our future prosperity.

1.20 As consumers we all want higher living standards and a better quality of life: better hospitals and schools; a cleaner environment; great museums and art galleries; world class sporting facilities and everything else that is civilised in our society. Our living standards and quality of life are not entitlements; they depend ultimately on the ability of firms throughout the economy to create jobs, improve productivity and to win business in home and overseas markets. Success has to be earned through improved competitiveness.

WHAT IS COMPETITIVENESS?

Our success, and ultimately our standard of living, will depend on continuously improving all aspects of our performance across the whole economy.

For a firm, competitiveness is the ability to produce the right goods and services of the right quality, at the right price, at the right time. It means meeting customers' needs more efficiently and more effectively than other firms.

For a nation, the OECD defines competitiveness as:

"...the degree to which it can, under free and fair market conditions, produce goods and services which meet the test of international markets, while simultaneously maintaining and expanding the real incomes of its people over the long term."

A sustained improvement in our competitiveness requires further underlying improvement in long term productivity, control of costs, and a performance in many aspects of national life that compares favourably with others.

Trade has been a major engine of world growth. An open world economy provides the opportunities to specialise and reap economies of scale. It also provides the stimulus of competition. There are prizes in world markets for all.

Other nations are determined to improve their competitiveness.

1.21 Others recognise the importance of competitiveness. The European Commission has recently published a White Paper[1]. Germany has also published a report[2]. The US, Canada, Australia and New Zealand all regard competitiveness as a key issue. The fast growing countries in the Far East already know that it is vital to economic success.

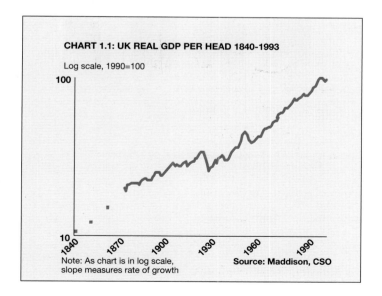

CHART 1.1: UK REAL GDP PER HEAD 1840-1993

Log scale, 1990=100

Note: As chart is in log scale, slope measures rate of growth

Source: Maddison, CSO

We must do the same or continue our long standing relative decline.

1.22 The first indications of weakness in our long run performance were recognised over 100 years ago. Manufacturing productivity grew by less than 1 per cent a year between 1890 and 1914. Although UK firms caught up in some industries in the inter war years, notably in chemicals, petroleum and motor vehicles, key weaknesses remained.

1.23 After 1945 our standard of living rose faster than ever before (chart 1.1). But other countries did still better. Countries such as Germany, France and Italy caught up and then overtook us. By the

---

[1] Commission of the European Communities; *Growth, Competitiveness, Employment: The Challenges and Ways Forward into the 21st Century.* [COM (93) 700] (1993)

[2] *Report of the Federal Government on the safeguarding of Germany's future as an industrial location* [Federal Government] (1993)

late 1970s, the UK suffered from high and seemingly chronic inflation. Strikes were common. Increased Government intervention distorted decision taking. Protected industries were unable to adjust to changing world conditions. Profitability was low, productivity levels fell further behind those of our competitors, output grew slowly and the gap in living standards between the UK and our major competitors widened.

Our competitiveness improved markedly during the 1980s...

1.24 The Government came to power in 1979 determined to reverse the long term decline in our relative economic performance by tackling fundamental weaknesses. Our underlying competitive position improved during the 1980s:

- manufacturing productivity grew faster in the UK than in the US, France and Germany (chart 1.2);

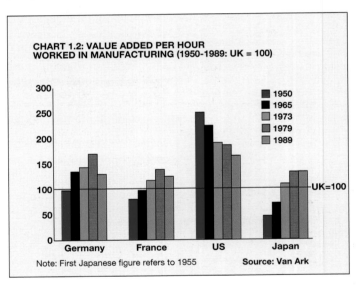

- our share of the volume of world trade in manufactures stabilised after decades of decline (chart 1.3);

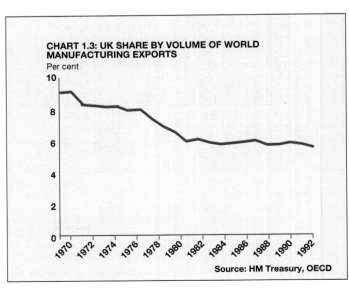

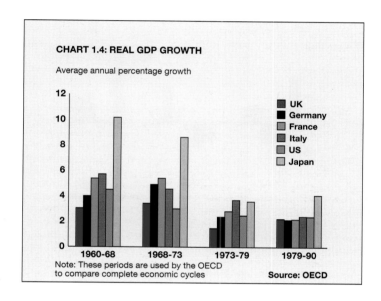

CHART 1.4: REAL GDP GROWTH

Average annual percentage growth

Legend: UK, Germany, France, Italy, US, Japan

Note: These periods are used by the OECD to compare complete economic cycles

Source: OECD

- our overall growth rate was similar to that in France, Germany and Italy, whereas we had grown significantly more slowly in previous economic cycles (chart 1.4);

- employment rose by over 1¼ million over the last economic cycle, faster than at any time for at least 30 years;

- the climate of industrial relations was transformed. Working days lost in 1993 were the lowest since records began 100 years ago;

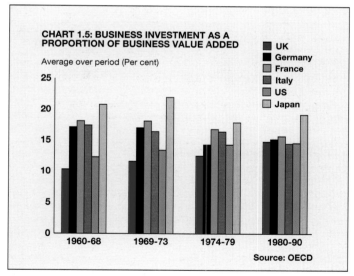

CHART 1.5: BUSINESS INVESTMENT AS A PROPORTION OF BUSINESS VALUE ADDED

Average over period (Per cent)

Legend: UK, Germany, France, Italy, US, Japan

Source: OECD

- the business sector invested a similar proportion of its value added to our major competitors after lagging behind in previous cycles (chart 1.5);

- we succeeded in attracting the lion's share of US and Japanese investment in the EC in the 1980s; and

- there was a dramatic rise in the number of small firms – at the end of 1991 there were around 900,000 more small businesses than in 1979 – and in self employment (chart 1.6).

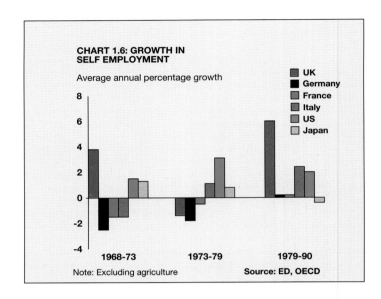

SMALL FIRMS

Small firms play a vital role in the economy. They are flexible and responsive to change. They stimulate competition and are a major source of job creation. They play a significant role in innovation. They contribute to flexible procurement from out-sourcing and sub contracting.

- *96 per cent of businesses employ fewer than 20 people, representing one third of the private sector workforce*
- *During the 1980s the small firms sector grew at a faster rate in the UK than in the rest of Europe, Japan, and the US*
- *Between 1989 and 1991 (the most recent figures) small firms created an additional 350,000 jobs*

The Government is encouraging the growth of the small firms sector through:

- *well targeted tax reliefs*
- *deregulation*
- *help with finance*
- *help with information and advice*
- *help with consultancy and management best practice*
- *help with business and skills training*

We need many more small firms to grow into medium and large enterprises. Business Links in England, and equivalent measures elsewhere, will assist here.

... yet the search for competitiveness is never ending.

1.25 It is an enormous task to correct over 100 years of relative decline. The improvements of the 1980s mean that we are now back in touch with the leaders, but there remains a lot of ground to make up.

1.26 Although we have many world beating companies, average productivity levels in manufacturing have not yet risen to those of our major competitors:

- a comparison of productivity levels in the economy as a whole and in manufacturing (chart 1.7) suggests that our productivity shortfall is less in services;

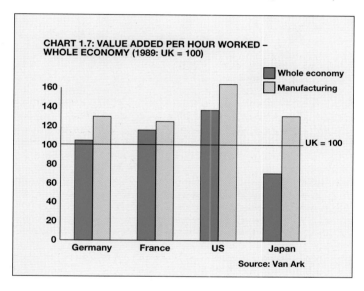

CHART 1.7: VALUE ADDED PER HOUR WORKED – WHOLE ECONOMY (1989: UK = 100)

Source: Van Ark

- our financial services sector is a major export earner (chart 1.8). According to British Invisibles, gross earnings by the City, including interest, profits and dividends, amounted to some £18.8 billion in 1992;

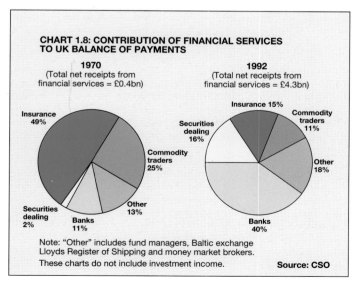

CHART 1.8: CONTRIBUTION OF FINANCIAL SERVICES TO UK BALANCE OF PAYMENTS

1970
(Total net receipts from financial services = £0.4bn)

Insurance 49%
Securities dealing 2%
Banks 11%
Other 13%
Commodity traders 25%

1992
(Total net receipts from financial services = £4.3bn)

Insurance 15%
Securities dealing 16%
Commodity traders 11%
Other 18%
Banks 40%

Note: "Other" includes fund managers, Baltic exchange Lloyds Register of Shipping and money market brokers.
These charts do not include investment income.

Source: CSO

- our overall share of world trade in services has continued to fall (chart 1.9); and

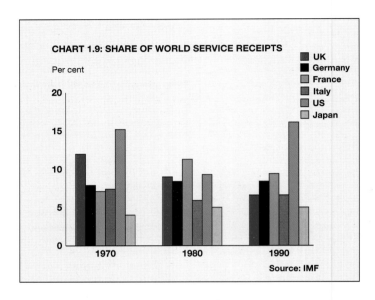

- our GDP per head remains below that of many other advanced countries (chart 1.10).

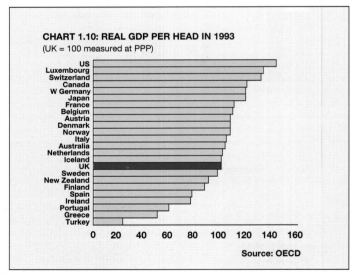

All sectors of the economy are important.

1.27 A competitive manufacturing sector is essential for our long term prosperity. The share of manufacturing in total output has fallen over time in the UK and in other major economies. But manufacturing is a major employer and its output, more than that of any other sector, is tested on international markets. A 1 per cent change in exports of manufactures would be balanced by a 3 per cent change in the exports of services.

1.28 A competitive service sector is also vital. The service sector accounts for around two thirds of total output and employs well over 16 million people. World trade in services is growing more quickly than trade in goods. Many of today's high technology industries are in the service sector and are driving research in new products. For example, the needs of the health industry shape the research of pharmaceutical companies.

1.29 Manufacturing and services are also increasingly interlinked. Many manufacturing businesses are contracting out activities such as marketing and computing. The success of manufacturing industry therefore depends on an efficient service sector. Moreover, as manufacturing products become more complex, they contain an increasing service element, whose performance is vital to success.

The Government is determined to help UK business to succeed.

1.30 Businesses – not governments – create wealth. The primary responsibility for improving competitiveness must lie with firms. The Government's role is to create the conditions in which firms throughout the economy can improve competitiveness by:

- providing the stable macroeconomic environment which enables business to plan ahead with confidence;

- making markets work more efficiently, and broadening the influence of market disciplines on resource allocation;

- pursuing tax policies which encourage enterprise and do not hinder economic efficiency; and

- improving value for money in those services which are best provided by the public sector.

1.31 The Government must provide the legal framework of property rights, laws of contract and so on, which markets require if they are to work well. Regulation may sometimes be needed to reproduce the effect of markets in natural monopolies or to reduce uncertainty, but over-regulation stifles innovation, restricts consumer choice, and imposes undue burdens on companies.

1.32 The Government must ensure that competition is fostered and that monopolies do not develop which are against the public interest. UK firms with world beating products need access to world markets and UK consumers – including firms seeking suppliers – need access to the best that the rest of the world can offer. Competition should be fair, so that consumers are properly informed and protected, access to markets is not artificially obstructed, and prices are not distorted by subsidies.

1.33 Often the Government can help most by getting out of the way. In the 1970s the State ran the phone company and the main airline. It manufactured cars and steel and ran a high street bank. Privatisation has expanded the market sector, transferring the ownership of almost 50 major businesses to the private sector where efficiency has been improved by market disciplines.

ACHIEVEMENTS OF PRIVATISATION

Since 1979 almost two-thirds of the industries then under state control and nearly 1 million public sector jobs have been transferred to the private sector.

*These changes have brought substantial benefits for **consumers**. The price of telephone calls has fallen by more than 30 per cent in real terms since BT was privatised. The UK water industry has been able to invest £5 billion in improving the standards of drinking and bathing water much sooner than could have been achieved in the public sector.*

***Lower prices, greater innovation and higher levels of service** provided by the privatised companies are helping to raise the competitiveness of other UK companies. For example, the average price charged to most of British Gas's industrial customers has fallen by over 30 per cent in real terms since privatisation.*

*The privatised industries are major **exporters and overseas investors**, generating substantial sales and revenue for the UK.*

***Taxpayers** have also gained. In 1979 the nationalised industries cost the taxpayer £50 million a week. In 1992/93 those companies that had been privatised paid almost £60 million a week to the Exchequer, mainly in corporation tax.*

1.34 Where markets do not work well in delivering the goods and services that people want, the Government has a positive and proactive role to play. It has a central role in areas critical to the process of wealth creation.

1.35 The provision of good quality education is essential to the creation of an opportunity society in which everyone has an equal chance of fulfilling their potential. The funding of research and development helps to develop the country's knowledge base and technological advantage. The Government can also address wider structural issues such as the supply of capital to small firms, remove barriers to employment and encourage employers to train their workforces. The Government's role in maintaining law and order is also fundamental to the development of a society in which business can flourish.

1.36 Government activity has to be financed. A broad tax base, with a simple structure, and low marginal rates, does the least harm to enterprise and work effort.

1.37 Public services should be delivered efficiently. Government itself need not be a large-scale provider. Market testing the delivery of services, and contracting out where appropriate, brings commercial disciplines to bear and stimulates private sector activity. The Private Finance Initiative (PFI) is breaking down the traditional barriers between private and public sectors, applying enterprise in activities which cannot be wholly privatised.

PRIVATE FINANCE INITIATIVE

The PFI seeks to develop new partnerships between the public and private sectors to the benefit of both. It:

- *aims to harness the private sector's ingenuity and management expertise, as well as bringing additional resources to bear*
- *offers a new approach to investment in a whole range of activities and services traditionally regarded as the exclusive domain of the public sector*
- *encourages efficient and economical ways of delivering more quickly the improved infrastructure and better facilities we all want to see*
- *means new business opportunities for the private sector, based on its existing strength and expertise*

There are no hard and fast rules on how the PFI operates for individual projects, although where there are joint ventures the private sector should be in control. The Government is looking for innovative solutions, in ways that properly share the risks with the private sector, and give value for money to the taxpayer.

Sir Alastair Morton chairs a Private Finance Panel made up of senior representatives from both the private and public sectors. The Panel acts as a catalyst to promote individual projects within the Initiative.

Since the launch of the PFI in November 1992:

- *it has been announced that projects worth over £6 billion are expected to proceed*
- *a competition has been launched to select a joint venture partner for the Channel Tunnel Rail Link*
- *other transport projects named as potential joint ventures between the public and private sectors include the Docklands Light Railway extension to Lewisham, the modernisation of the West Coast Main Line and Crossrail*
- *a decision has been taken to let contracts for roads which will be designed, built, financed and operated by the private sector*
- *the private sector is providing a growing number of services to the NHS, and is being invited to finance, design, construct and run new prisons*

Other Government policies attract significant private finance into areas such as housing, urban development and education. Such funding is equally subject to private sector disciplines, to everyone's benefit in terms of the efficient use of resources.

Government must act in partnership with business.

1.38 Every day, the Government – at all levels – takes hundreds of decisions which affect business. It negotiates internationally, makes laws, applies regulations, helps firms export, buys goods and services, and decides how much tax to raise. To carry out these functions efficiently, the Government needs to understand fully how businesses work, appreciate the problems they face and take account of how its actions affect them. On many issues businesses and Government will have a common interest in finding solutions that enhance our competitiveness.

1.39 This partnership requires detailed understanding and appreciation of business needs across all sectors of the economy. Government action needs to be directed at making markets work better, helping business to help itself through better informed decisions and spreading best practice. Above all, it must help companies to become more competitive and thus to sell successfully in domestic and world markets.

The task ahead.

1.40 There are no short cuts to improving competitiveness. We need a long term commitment from everyone – individuals, companies, and Government – to improvement across a broad front. All of the factors behind the UK's long term relative underperformance need to be addressed. This White Paper sets out the Government's proposals.

1.41 A stable **macroeconomy** – based on low inflation and sound public finances – gives business the confidence to undertake the investment which is essential for wealth creation. High inflation increases uncertainty, shortens time horizons and imposes other costs on business and households.

1.42 Europe is an important determinant of UK competitiveness. The Government is working to improve European competitiveness.

1.43 Further improvement in **education and training** is a key requirement. Raising the average level of attainment and greater access to education are vital for competitiveness. In future, the most successful nations will be those which develop high quality, skilled and motivated workforces and make good use of them.

1.44 The **labour market** needs to match demand and supply for labour and skills. It needs to react flexibly to new patterns of work and changing technological requirements. High levels of structural unemployment waste resources and damage the fabric of society.

1.45 The need for businesses to remain internationally competitive involves commitment to continuous **innovation**. Improved performance in innovation – the commercial exploitation of new ideas – through successful **management** is vital. The Government is playing its part by attaching the highest priority to wealth creation in its own funding of science and technology.

1.46 Fair and open markets provide the spur to enterprise and improved efficiency by matching UK producers against the world's best. Inward investment benefits the domestic economy. Outward investment can help firms to exploit opportunities elsewhere.

1.47 Businesses need capital to grow. The availability of **finance** is therefore vital. Modern and efficient **communications and infrastructure** are needed to help businesses get their goods and services quickly and efficiently to their customers. Through the PFI the Government is seeking to involve the private sector to a greater extent than in the past. **Regeneration** improves the competitiveness of firms, the job prospects and quality of life of local people, and the social and physical environment.

1.48 The **commercial framework** sets the climate for wealth creation. A domestic environment that favours deregulation, whilst respecting essential standards, enables companies to respond quickly to the marketplace. The prime purpose of **taxation** is to fund public services but a burdensome regime can stifle growth.

1.49 Finally, the **business of government** must be carried out efficiently and effectively otherwise industry will not get the support it needs. Tight control of public spending is essential if sound public finances are to be achieved while keeping tax rates as low as possible. The public sector is by far the largest purchaser of goods and services in the UK. Good **purchasing** can have a profound effect on the competitiveness of firms.

THE MACROECONOMIC FRAMEWORK

2.1 The Government's overall economic objective is to promote sustained economic growth and higher living standards by ensuring that markets work properly and establishing a stable macroeconomic environment for business.

2.2 A successful macroeconomic policy is central to competitiveness. Business needs a stable framework if it is to invest for the future and develop the products and services on which our prosperity depends. That means low inflation and the interest rates that go with it. Past failures to deliver low inflation on a sustained basis and problems with the public finances have stifled previous recoveries and have added to the risks that businesses face.

2.3 But the successful conduct of fiscal and monetary policy cannot generate sustained economic growth on its own. Increased prosperity depends on the efforts of individuals and firms throughout the economy and on the improvements in the supply side of the economy which are addressed throughout this White Paper.

Macroeconomic stability is important...

2.4 Risk is an inescapable feature of business life. But firms will be more willing to undertake projects which provide returns in the medium or long term if they can be reasonably confident of sustained and steady growth of aggregate demand. All governments, particularly those in open economies like our own, recognise that they cannot completely avoid the business cycle. But governments have to avoid adding to instability.

2.5 History shows that lasting changes to levels of employment and the growth of living standards cannot be achieved by stimulating demand through fiscal and monetary expansion. Such attempts led ultimately to higher inflation and weaker economic performance. Jobs were destroyed, not created, as policy had to be tightened. Attempts to offset the consequences of macroeconomic policy errors through, for example, prices and incomes policies, made matters worse by harming incentives. Artificially stimulated growth simply disguised structural weakness in the economy.

... based on low inflation...

2.6 Low inflation - and, most importantly, the confidence that inflation will be kept low - is essential for better economic performance and improved competitiveness:

- inflation harms markets by distorting price signals. Changes in relative prices become confused with general inflationary increases. Even with just 5 per cent annual inflation, prices double every 14 years, swamping most relative price changes;

- high inflation creates uncertainty, the enemy of growth and investment. If businesses are unsure about future prices and inflation, and hence about real interest rates and future returns, they will be less willing to take risks and invest, particularly in long-term projects. Inflation encourages an emphasis on short-term profit at the expense of longer term returns;

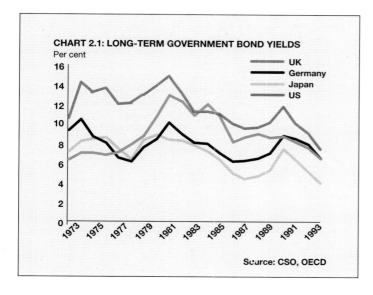

CHART 2.1: LONG-TERM GOVERNMENT BOND YIELDS
Per cent

UK
Germany
Japan
US

Source: CSO, OECD

- inflation pushes up interest rates (chart 2.1). High nominal interest rates impose heavy demands for cash flows in the early years of a project's life, increasing the risk of failure in difficult times. This too may encourage "short-termism";

- fear of inflation makes matters worse. Savers and lenders require a premium to protect themselves against the risk of inflation eroding the value of their loans, raising nominal and real interest rates. These fears mean that to reduce this premium, inflation has to be kept low on a permanent basis;

- high and uncertain inflation means that people spend time trying to insure against or avoid its consequences. Time that could be better used in creating wealth; and

- inflation adds to social tension by redistributing income and wealth in arbitrary and unjust ways.

... and sound public finances.

2.7 If a government cannot keep its own finances in order, it adds to the uncertainty that businesses face. The risk of unsustainably large deficits makes it more difficult to operate monetary policy. High levels of government borrowing increase the burden of public debt, raising interest rates and ultimately forcing higher taxes or cuts in public spending.

The Government is determined to keep inflation down...

2.8 In the 1970s, the UK's inflation rate was too high, and much higher than most of our competitors (chart 2.2). Prices more than trebled. High inflation went hand in hand with volatile inflation, increasing uncertainty. Breaking the inflationary psychology was difficult and painful, and the success in reducing inflation in the 1980s was only partial.

2.9 The Government is determined to maintain permanently low inflation. It has set a target range of 1-4 per cent for underlying inflation and aims to bring it down to the lower half of the range by the end of the current Parliament. To help achieve this a number of changes has been made to increase the consistency and transparency of monetary policy.

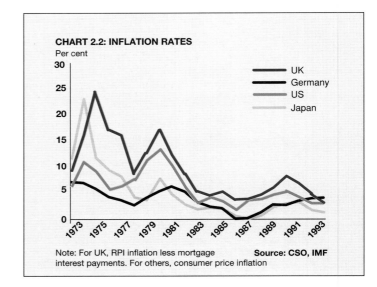

CHART 2.2: INFLATION RATES
Per cent

Note: For UK, RPI inflation less mortgage interest payments. For others, consumer price inflation

Source: CSO, IMF

2.10 This framework has so far proved successful. Underlying inflation has stayed within the target range since October 1992, and compares favourably with inflation in other industrial countries. Earnings growth has been at its lowest level for 25 years. This progress has been achieved while short-term interest rates have been cut and against the background of a steady economic recovery.

2.11 The Government recognises that fluctuating exchange rates add to the risks faced by business. Exchange rate stability is particularly important within the EC to obtain the full benefits of the Single Market. The Government believes that the best immediate route to exchange rate stability in Europe is through the common pursuit of policies to achieve low inflation and sound public finances in all European economies. This coincides with the interests of the UK and UK business.

2.12 The UK's price competitiveness depends fundamentally on improving productivity and controlling our costs. Policies directed at permanently low inflation and competitive markets provide the best environment in which to achieve this. The 1970s demonstrated that a policy of continued devaluation only raises inflation and is damaging to long-run economic success.

... and restore sound public finances.

2.13 Borrowing inevitably rises when the economy is in recession. Tax revenues fall and public spending rises because of higher outlays on benefits and public services. Allowing borrowing to rise in these circumstances also helps to stabilise the economy. But the resulting high borrowing requirements in the last recession added rapidly to public sector debt and threatened unacceptable rises in the debt interest burden in many developed countries.

2.14 Once recovery was clearly under way in the UK, borrowing needed to be reduced sharply. In the two Budgets of 1993 it was necessary to take tough decisions to restore the health of public finances. Tax increases were inevitable but tight control of public spending - which will fall as a share of GDP through time - has ensured and will ensure that tax rates are kept as low as possible. Public borrowing will fall as the Budget measures come into effect and as the economy recovers.

2.15 The spending plans announced in the November 1993 Budget reflected the Government's determination to pursue priorities which contribute to an improved economic performance over the longer term. The new plans increased the funds for education and training, maintained the real level of the science budget, helped exporters by increasing export credit cover and reducing premiums, and gave greater emphasis to the PFI. Savings were made elsewhere in the Government's spending plans.

Macroeconomic policy on its own is not enough.

2.16 Competitiveness is not simply the result of pulling macroeconomic levers. Competitiveness depends on the efficiency of the real economy. The steps that the Government has taken to bring down inflation and restore sound public finances will provide the essential macroeconomic environment in which industry and commerce can meet the competitive challenge.

THE EUROPEAN DIMENSION

Post War renewal

3.1 The post-war generation of European statesmen focused on two priorities: the reconstruction of societies and economies ravaged by war; and the creation of cooperative European institutions designed to prevent another war. The European Coal and Steel Community, EURATOM and the European Economic Community were the chosen vehicles.

3.2 For the citizens of Europe the contrast between the 1950s and the 1990s is enormous. Living standards have been transformed. While relative prosperity was restored on the back of post-war reconstruction, few foresaw the economic challenge that was to undermine so many of the assumptions of the 1950s.

3.3 Improving standards of living was an EC objective from the start, laid down in the Treaty of Rome. The delivery mechanisms were free movement of goods, people, services and capital, and measures to avoid distortion of competition.

3.4 And yet the Community underachieved. The competition rules were barely exploited; liberalising regulations took decades to agree and state aids flourished. In the late 1970s, "Eurosclerosis" was diagnosed. Europe was exposed to a surge of competitive challenges. Rising unemployment threatened living standards.

The Single Market

3.5 The Community needed reinvigorating – a new approach to competing in the world. The prescription which the UK helped promote was the Single Market. A systematic attempt was made to remove barriers, harmonise standards, and open up the national markets of Western Europe to a different scale of competitive pressure. The use of qualified majority voting, introduced by the Single European Act, made rapid agreement on market opening measures possible.

3.6 Within the EC, Lord Cockfield masterminded the daunting task of implementing the Single Market agenda. Nearly 300 different sets of national rules had to be negotiated into common measures. This was bound to lead to indigestion as citizens and companies were subjected to a bewildering process of change. Furthermore, in some cases, the legislative consequences were over-prescriptive. They affected everyday life in ways that were sometimes incomprehensible, when compared to the fundamental purpose of creating a single market of 340 million people – 370 million now that the European Economic Area is in place – and the accession negotiations with four EFTA countries are complete. Yet further potential is offered by the agreements with Central and Eastern European countries which are intended to lead to their entry to the EC.

The UK in the Single Market

3.7 The benefits of the Single Market for UK prosperity and competitiveness are:

- increased consumer choice;

- removal of barriers to trade through mutual recognition of standards, and harmonisation where appropriate;

- liberalisation of public procurement;

- the right to trade financial services throughout the EC on the basis of a single authorisation 'passport';

- mutual recognition of professional and vocational qualifications; and

- reduction in bureaucracy, for example: 60 million fewer official border check forms each year in the Community, 9 to 10 million fewer in the UK; abolition of the Single Administrative Document saving UK business £135 million a year; commercial freight passing straight through borders.

These benefits more than compensate for the discomfort of change.

3.8 Creating a genuine Single Market is not just about legislation. Distortions to competition can also be created by subsidies to companies, by lack of transparency in public ownership or by anti-competitive practices in business. The UK has been very active in pressing the Commission to use its powers in the Treaty of Rome to tackle these distortions.

3.9 Business is benefitting from the manufacturing and marketing efficiencies offered by the Single Market which is now the main focus of our trade (chart 3.1).

3.10 The Single Market also attracts investment to the UK – from within the EC and from outside – and the UK has done particularly well.

Developing the Single Market

3.11 We are far from realising the full benefits of the Single Market. Further liberalisation is needed, for example, in aviation, energy and telecommunications. Not all measures have reached their entry into force date and the Market must be "run in". This needs proper and even enforcement and action to tackle continuing

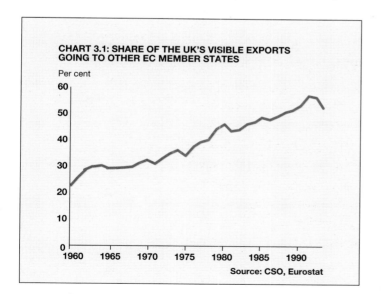

CHART 3.1: SHARE OF THE UK'S VISIBLE EXPORTS GOING TO OTHER EC MEMBER STATES

Per cent

Source: CSO, Eurostat

barriers. The Government is working hard with the Commission and other Member States to ensure efficient cooperation between administrations to achieve transparency of enforcement methods so that problems can be solved swiftly. DTI's Single Market Compliance Unit assists business in tackling illegal barriers and is discussing with the Commission ways of improving Community complaints procedures. In parallel the Government must ensure that the European Council's commitment to rigorous application of the competition and state aid rules is fulfilled.

3.12 The Government will continue to press the Commission to remove excessive burdens on industry. Single Market directives have been introduced to replace a confusion of numerous national regulations. But in some cases EC legislation has been too detailed and burdensome. Increasingly the focus is on minimising Community regulation required to ensure free movement; leaving maximum leeway to Member States in accordance with the principle of subsidiarity; and in relying where possible on mutual recognition of national systems.

3.13 The Single Market is the Community's most impressive achievement and is already making a significant contribution to competitiveness. Substantial Government effort has been put into its negotiation and is being devoted to its upkeep.

3.14 Other Community policies can also contribute to competitiveness, most obviously the research and development (R&D) Framework Programme for promoting innovation, the Structural Funds for regional regeneration and Trans-European Networks for improving infrastructure. In all these areas it is essential to appraise and evaluate projects fully in order to ensure that Community money is spent cost-effectively and directed at real needs.

The International Challenge

3.15 Improving the Community's internal competitiveness is essential, but not enough. Although Europe is the UK's most important market we cannot focus solely on meeting European standards of competitiveness. We need to compete with the rest of the world. Some of our fiercest competitors now come from Asia. Average hourly labour costs in manufacturing in the four Asian "Tigers" are much lower than in Europe. And a generally high standard of education and training has enabled these countries progressively to move up the technology ladder. This change in comparative advantage has increased competition in some markets. At the same time, increasing prosperity in Asia is opening up opportunities for European exporters. The Community has been slow to react. It must now respond to the challenge.

Community Social Policy

3.16 Some Community policies risk damaging our competitiveness. The Government supports Treaty objectives for social, environmental and consumer protection. What the Government cannot accept is legislation which imposes vastly increased costs and rigidities and makes it harder to safeguard existing jobs or create new ones. The Government does not agree that harmonisation of employment law and social provisions is necessary for the operation of the Single Market. For this reason the Government was not prepared to sign up to the social chapter proposed at Maastricht and secured the assurance, provided by the Social Protocol, that legislation agreed by the other eleven Member States would not apply to the UK. In this way it has succeeded in resisting the application of the proposed Works Council Directive to firms in the UK. The Government supports voluntary employee involvement but it should not be imposed in a single pan-European regulatory framework which fails to take account of the differing needs of modern businesses.

THE COSTS OF SOCIAL PROTECTION

The costs of public social protection – social security, social assistance and health care – are high in Europe compared with our main competitors. They were equivalent to 26 per cent of GDP in the EC in 1990, compared with 15 per cent in the US, 12 per cent in Japan and 23 per cent in the UK.

In most European countries, employers bear a far larger share of the costs than in the UK:

- in Germany employers contributed 41 per cent of total social protection funding in 1990, compared with 27 per cent in the UK, while French and Italian employers contributed 52 and 53 per cent respectively.
- in 1992 UK manufacturing non-wage costs – mainly employers' social security, pensions and health insurance contributions – were 17 per cent of total labour costs, compared with 23 per cent in the US and Germany, 29 per cent in France and 31 per cent in Italy and Sweden.

Manufacturing non-wage costs were only 13 per cent of labour costs in Japan, 11 per cent in Korea and 7 per cent in Taiwan.

3.17 The Community's social policy is at an important turning point. In its response[1] to the Commission Green Paper[2] on the future of social policy, the Government has pressed for a sensible programme of action which helps Member States to tackle unemployment and promote competitiveness. The Government wants to ensure that the people of Europe enjoy the benefits of the Single Market. If our partners favour proposals that raise business costs, then the Social Protocol route is open to them.

[1] *European Commission Green Paper on European Social Policy: The UK response.* [Employment Department] (1994)

[2] *European Commission Green Paper: European Social Policy Options for the Union.* [COM 93/551] (1993)

The Commission's White Paper

3.18 The Commission's White Paper on Growth, Competitiveness and Employment[3] published last year is an important response to the competitiveness challenge. The conclusions agreed at the Brussels European Council provide an action plan for both Member States and the Community and a commitment to monitor its implementation. The action plan encompasses a wide range of activities, from macroeconomic stability to R&D, from Trans-European Networks to an open trade policy. There is welcome recognition of the UK's agenda of deregulation, structural reform and the need for flexible labour markets.

The Right Economic Climate

3.19 With increased market integration it makes sense to coordinate economic and monetary policies in Europe providing these share the UK's objective of low inflation and a disciplined management of our economy. The Council of Ministers and the European Monetary Institute provide the fora for that coordination and cooperation. The Government also supports convergence, which is important for exchange rate stability. Some countries see convergence leading inevitably to a single currency. This is conjecture. The UK's opt-out preserves the right of Parliament to decide when and if we should join the move to a single currency.

The UK's Agenda

3.20 The UK's agenda for enhancing European competitiveness includes:

- a stable macroeconomic climate;

- a more efficient and market-orientated Common Agricultural Policy;

- an open and fair trade policy;

- strict application of the state aids and competition rules;

- supporting effective programmes on R&D, infrastructure and regional funds;

- systematic reviews of the burden on business of Community legislation, deregulating where necessary, and avoiding new burdens;

- encouraging privatisation and the break-up of uncompetitive and inefficient monopolies;

[3] Commission of the European Communities; *Growth, Competitiveness, Employment: The Challenges and Ways Forward into the 21st Century.* [COM (93) 700] (1993)

- proper and even implementation and enforcement of Single Market and other rules;

- encouraging job creation by restraining non-wage costs and encouraging flexible work patterns; and

- focusing Community programmes on the real needs of industry and ensuring value for money.

3.21 Policy towards Europe and policy on competitiveness cannot be separated. Europe affects our competitiveness across the board. It is in our national self-interest to press for a genuinely competitive market place. The Single Market and GATT experience show how the UK's voice can be critically important in influencing European – and World – policy. That is why we must be at the heart of Europe, participating fully in discussions that affect our national interests and our national prosperity.

EDUCATION AND TRAINING

4.1 Hard working people with high skills, and the knowledge and understanding to use them to the full, are the lifeblood of a modern, internationally competitive economy. We have to aim higher than in the past. We have to develop the self confidence and self esteem which make good citizens and good workers. We have to demand respect and rewards for vocational education and training as well as academic study. Above all, we have to give all our people – not just some of them – every opportunity to give of their best, from their very first day at school to the end of their working lives. A fulfilled workforce meeting individual targets, driven by the will to perform to their individual best, will be a world class workforce.

4.2 For too long the UK's levels of participation and achievement have dragged us down the international education and training league. The economist Alfred Marshall recognised the gap with Germany, Scandinavia and Switzerland shortly after the First World War. In 1970 international comparisons indicated that twice as many people in the UK were weak at science as in Germany. Our mathematics students were even further behind their international counterparts in 1980 than they were in 1964. The Government and its partners – employers, schools, colleges and other trainers, and learners themselves – are now beginning to close the gap again. But there is much still to do.

4.3 The Government is working to lever up the expectations of students and providers alike; to strengthen standards of teaching, learning and assessment; to promote more effective training by employers; and to foster a culture of lifetime learning and flexibility.

4.4 But the UK Government is not alone in recognising the importance of good quality education and training. Across the globe other countries are setting ever higher standards for the educational and training attainment of their workforce, and benefiting from the boost to competitiveness that this provides. And the pace of change is quickening.

4.5 As a nation, therefore, we must aim higher and achieve even more. While we are second to none in securing results from those in our society who choose the most academic options, we need to raise further the attainment of those, whatever their age, who choose vocational education and training.

The Government's Approach

4.6 Since 1979 the Government has introduced a series of major reforms to boost the outputs from our education and training system. Schools and colleges have been galvanised by a new emphasis on choice, quality and sharp accountability for results. In parallel, the Government has encouraged employers to take responsibility for the training and development of their workforce, now and for the future. Training and Enterprise Councils (TECs); in Scotland, Local Enterprise Companies (lecs); and Industry Training Organisations (ITOs) are playing an increasing role in identifying and meeting labour market needs. The Government has created a climate in which teachers, students and their parents, employers and their staff can act in partnership to:

- drive up participation, standards and attainment at all levels; and

- create a self-sustaining system where learning is part of the normal pattern of everyday life and work.

TRAINING AND ENTERPRISE COUNCILS

The 82 employer-led TECs in England and Wales are responsible for over £1.8 billion of public funding for training, vocational education and enterprise. Together with the lecs in Scotland, they play a role at local level in developing the skills of the workforce. Employers are also making significant financial contributions to the work of TECs.

The Government is introducing still higher standards for TECs to meet across a range of their activities. It is also gearing more funding (typically 25-40 per cent) to results, such as the qualifications and jobs gained by the 500,000 people who participate in their training programmes each year. Some TECs are piloting 100 per cent output-related funding.

NATIONAL TARGETS FOR EDUCATION AND TRAINING IN ENGLAND AND WALES

Foundation Learning

1   By 1997, 80 per cent of young people to reach National Vocational Qualification level 2 (NVQ2) (or equivalent, for example five GCSEs at grades A-C)
2   Training and education to NVQ3 (or equivalent for example two A levels, or a vocational A level) to be available to all young people who can benefit
3   By 2000, 50 per cent of young people to reach NVQ3 (or equivalent)
4   Education and training provision to develop self reliance, flexibility and breadth

Lifetime Learning

1   By 1996, all employees should take part in training or development activities
2   By 1996, 50 per cent of the workforce to be aiming for NVQs or units towards them
3   By 2000, 50 per cent of the workforce to be qualified to at least NVQ3 (or equivalent)
4   By 1996, 50 per cent of medium-to-large organisations (200 or more employees) to be "Investors in People"

4.7 The National Targets for Education and Training, launched by the CBI and endorsed by the Government, now provide a focus for this partnership, and a challenge to do even better. As they become widely known they are beginning to act as a catalyst, stimulating employers, individuals and providers to raise their expectations and attainment. Already we are well on course to meet the Foundation Targets (chart 4.1). And in some sectors we are approaching Lifetime Targets 2 and 3 (chart 4.2).

4.8 The National Advisory Council for Education and Training Targets (NACETT) monitors progress toward the targets, and will shortly be reviewing them. The Government is asking NACETT to take full account of what the UK will need from its workforce to maintain and improve our competitiveness in the 21st century, and to consider the case for raising some of the targets to match our competitors' achievements. The Government looks forward to receiving NACETT's recommendations, including their advice on how best to manage the drive towards higher attainment. The Advisory Scottish Council on Education and Training Targets, encouraged by achievement in Scotland, has already launched challenging new Scottish targets which the Government has endorsed. Everyone must play their part. It is of vital importance that the targets are embedded in the national consciousness if we are to succeed, for only ambitious nations are successful nations.

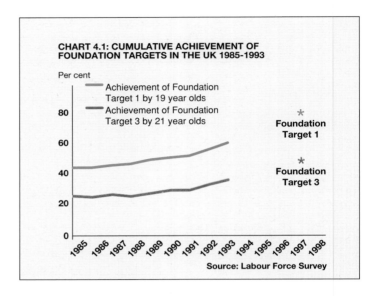

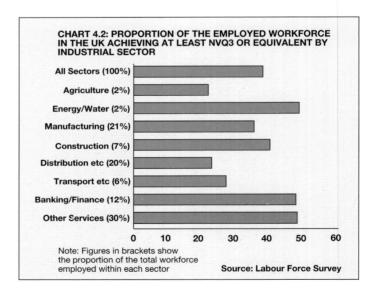

Good Schools

4.9 There is nothing inevitable about the success – or the failure – of a school. As the publication of performance tables and inspection reports has already demonstrated, results vary enormously. There are effective schools in areas of deprivation, and schools in the leafy suburbs which are not pulling their weight.

Success depends on the quality and commitment of head teachers and their staff, the cultivation of an ethos which emphasises hard work, self-discipline and high aspirations on the part of pupils, and the support shown by parents, employers and others in the local community. Every school should be aspiring to rise to the standards of the best.

4.10 The Government's reforms have done much to give schools the freedom to make the most of themselves and their pupils. But that must be accompanied by a sharp focus on teaching and learning, detailed information to enable parents and others to judge how well schools are doing, and mechanisms to identify failing schools and wherever possible put them right.

4.11 The National Curriculum in England and Wales remains at the heart of the Government's drive to raise quality and expectations in our schools, offering all young people a broad and balanced programme of education with demanding national standards for assessing pupils' progress. The independent Office for Standards in Education (OFSTED) has found that the National Curriculum is already raising standards and increasing motivation to learn, but its full impact will not be felt until children have followed it throughout their school career.

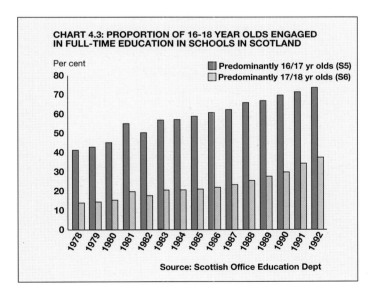

CHART 4.3: PROPORTION OF 16-18 YEAR OLDS ENGAGED IN FULL-TIME EDUCATION IN SCHOOLS IN SCOTLAND

Per cent

Predominantly 16/17 yr olds (S5)
Predominantly 17/18 yr olds (S6)

Source: Scottish Office Education Dept

4.12 In Scotland, major reforms to the curriculum for upper secondary education were announced in March 1994. They will be introduced from session 1997/8, to improve standards of attainment for the increasing numbers staying on at school (chart 4.3), build on recognised qualifications for all, maintain and develop breadth of study, and promote parity of esteem for vocational subjects. In Northern Ireland, a new curriculum was introduced in 1989. A review of the curriculum for 14-16 year olds is underway, including an examination of the need for more vocational options.

4.13 The Government is further strengthening the opportunities and incentives for schools to improve:

- OFSTED is ensuring rigorous regular inspections of the quality of teaching and learning. Its inspection reports, and similar reports by HM Inspectors in Scotland and Wales, and the Education and Training Inspectorate in Northern Ireland, are now made available to parents;

- the Government has introduced a mandatory Code of Practice to ensure consistency of GCSE examining;

- the Government is helping parents to make informed choices by publishing annual comparative performance tables for schools and colleges, including in particular the results achieved in public examinations. As soon as reliable measures are available, the value added by each school or college to its students' prior achievements will also be reported;

- information designed to spread good practice in schools will also be made available to governors and teachers. The Government is also working with local authorities, voluntary organisations and the business community to tackle truancy;

- Education Associations now stand ready to tackle schools which prove unable to meet the required quality standards. Such schools will be taken over temporarily or, if necessary, closed; and

- later this year a copy of the Parent's Charter will be sent to every household in England. This will tell parents about the reforms in schools and their rights to high quality education for their children. Updated Parent's Charters will also be issued in Wales and Scotland.

4.14 Greater choice is a further stimulus to improvement. There are now over 900 self-governing (grant maintained (GM)) schools, with another 150 in the pipeline. A Funding Agency for Schools has been established in England to support GM schools. These schools are being encouraged to specialise in particular subjects, such as technology through the new network of technology colleges, as do the 15 City Technology Colleges. GM schools can now also consider introducing various types of selectivity in admission arrangements in response to local demand.

4.15 All this provides the context within which young people are steadily achieving more:

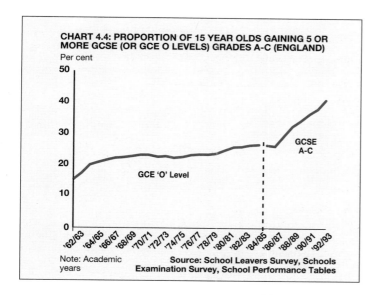

CHART 4.4: PROPORTION OF 15 YEAR OLDS GAINING 5 OR MORE GCSE (OR GCE O LEVELS) GRADES A-C (ENGLAND)

Per cent

GCSE A-C

GCE 'O' Level

Note: Academic years

Source: School Leavers Survey, Schools Examination Survey, School Performance Tables

- the proportion of pupils reaching compulsory school leaving age with 5 or more GCSEs at grades A*-C has risen, from 16 per cent in 1962/3 (or the GCE O level or CSE equivalent) to 41 per cent in 1993 (chart 4.4). When equivalent vocational qualifications are taken into account, 61 per cent of young people reached this level in 1993; and

- in Scotland the proportion of all school leavers with five or more Standard Grades in bands 1-3 rose from 39 per cent in 1981/2 to 49 per cent in 1991/2.

16-19: Helping Young Adults to Succeed

4.16 As they approach 16 and beyond, young adults need:

- high quality careers education and independent guidance to help them make the right choices;

- an understanding of the world of work;

- access to relevant, valued qualifications which harness their different aptitudes and ambitions; and

- a choice of high quality education and training options that meet both students' needs and those of employers.

4.17 Effective **careers education** prepares pupils for the choices they will make about future education, training and work. Most secondary schools now have a careers coordinator, a written policy statement, a good careers library and, in a growing number of cases, an agreement with the local Careers Service about the level of service they can expect.

4.18 Important reforms are under way in the Careers Service. The Service is being contracted out within a strong framework of standards and quality. Thirteen new local services, "Pathfinders", covering close to 20 per cent of the country, began operation in April 1994 and the remainder of the Service will be contracted out over the next two years. Parallel arrangements are being made in Scotland and Wales.

4.19 The Technical and Vocational Education Initiative (TVEI) has helped young people aged 14 to 18 to relate what they learn to the **world of work.** It equips them with broad based characteristics such as enterprise and initiative, and gives them valuable work experience.

4.20 Many companies provide schools with governors, advice, work experience and teacher placements, bringing business expertise and experience of work to schools. Many also provide financial support and help in kind. There is a steady growth in formal links between schools and business, notably through Education Business Partnerships, Compacts, and the Teacher Placement Service. In England:

- in 1991/2 92 per cent of secondary schools and 56 per cent of primary schools had links or contacts with local business; and

- 91 per cent of pupils in their last year of compulsory schooling were involved in work experience placements.

4.21 At 16, young people are able to choose between or combine courses leading to **three main types of qualification,** each enhancing the contribution they can make at work and opening up opportunities for further learning.

4.22 Traditional **GCE A Levels** have stood the test of time. The Government remains committed to them as a high quality option, particularly for those wishing to enter higher education. AS qualifications now provide a means of broadening GCE A level studies.

4.23 General National Vocational Qualifications (GNVQs) were introduced in September 1992. They will offer young people the opportunity to learn to high standards in a practical and vocational context. GNVQs prepare young people for employment in broad occupational areas, while also offering a route to higher education.

4.24 National Vocational Qualifications (NVQs) provide a guarantee to employers that the individual can perform a job in a particular occupation, to the specified level of skill and competence.

NEW QUALIFICATIONS FRAMEWORK

- *GCE **A levels** are tried and tested qualifications. The numbers of young people taking them, passing them, and passing them well, continues to rise: 26 per cent of 17 year olds now achieve two or more GCE A levels, compared with 14 per cent in 1980*

- *There are now 500 **NVQs** covering 150 occupations. These are applicable to more than 80 per cent of jobs. The CBI reports that 96 per cent of employers use NVQs or expect to benefit from them, while over 500,000 people have already attained NVQs*

- *Over 80,000 students are already pursuing **GNVQs**, and it is expected that around 50 per cent of 16-17 year-olds will be studying for them by 1996/7. Over 50 per cent of Scottish pupils in their third and fourth years of secondary schools are enrolled for National Certificate modules*

- *People should get credit for their existing vocational qualifications when they want to pursue academic qualifications and vice versa. The National Council for Vocational Qualifications **(NCVQ)** is working on this with higher education institutions and professional and employer bodies*

- *In **Scotland** three main types of qualification will also be available: SCE Standard Grades and Highers (and from 1998/9 Advanced Highers), general Scottish Vocational Qualifications (GSVQs) and Scottish Vocational Qualifications (SVQs). In Scotland the percentage of all leavers with three or more Highers rose to 28 per cent in 1991/2, compared with 21 per cent in 1986/7*

4.25 Students now have a wide range of study options, full-time or part-time, at 16 and beyond. Many stay at on at school in the **sixth form.** Others move into the **further education sector –** further education colleges, tertiary colleges and sixth form colleges. These have been given new freedoms and flexibility in running their own affairs. The sector is funded by the Further Education Funding Councils (FEFC) for England and Wales. The colleges play a key part in meeting the needs of employers, young people and adults for high quality general and vocational education and training. The already extensive links between colleges and business are being strengthened, for example by the appointment of employer governors, and through the involvement of TECs.

PARTICIPATION IN EDUCATION AND TRAINING AT 16 AND 17

- *In 1993, 70 per cent of 16 year olds stayed on full-time in schools and colleges – compared to 42 per cent in 1979. Including those on YT or otherwise combining further study with work, well over 90 per cent of 16 year olds continued in some form of education or training (chart 4.5)*

- *Staying on rates among 17 year olds are improving. 54 per cent continued their studies full-time in 1992, double the proportion in 1979, and around 80 per cent were in some form of education or training*

- *A third of these 17 year olds now study for GCE A levels, and over 80 per cent pass (48 per cent at grades A-C). 26 per cent of 17 year olds now achieve two or more A levels compared to only 14 per cent in 1980 (chart 4.5)*

4.26 Participation in further education has grown substantially. The Government has provided for an expansion of close to 30 per cent in full-time equivalent student numbers between 1992/3 and 1996/7 (chart 4.6).

4.27 From this year, funding for the sector will be linked to the retention and achievements of its students. An additional demand-led element will encourage efficient growth. The FEFC's Inspectorate, which includes members with business experience, will regularly report on the quality of teaching and learning in each college. Details of qualifications achieved by FE students and what they do next are published and made available to all young people approaching the end of compulsory schooling.

4.28 Each college will be publishing its own charter this summer setting out how it intends to meet the requirements of the national Charter for Further Education. A new edition of the national Charter in 1995/6 will stimulate further improvement and identify good practice.

4.29 Youth Training (YT) continues to be the main training route for young people leaving school at age 16 or 17. A place is guaranteed to all young people unable to find a job, and there are also some 35 per cent of YT trainees with employed status. In 1992/3 50 per cent of those

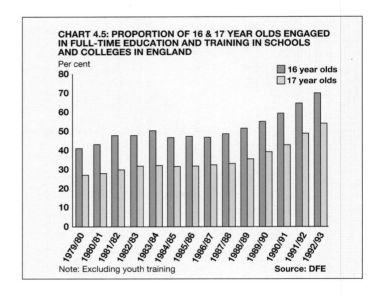

CHART 4.5: PROPORTION OF 16 & 17 YEAR OLDS ENGAGED IN FULL-TIME EDUCATION AND TRAINING IN SCHOOLS AND COLLEGES IN ENGLAND

Note: Excluding youth training   Source: DFE

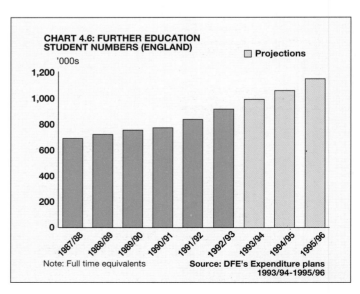

CHART 4.6: FURTHER EDUCATION STUDENT NUMBERS (ENGLAND)

Note: Full time equivalents   Source: DFE's Expenditure plans 1993/94-1995/96 leaving YT gained a qualification or a credit towards one, mainly at NVQ Level 2 or higher. The proportion is expected to rise to 65 per cent in 1996/7.

4.30 There is still a need for more skilled people at technician and modern craft level. The Government is working with employers, TECs and ITOs to introduce **"Modern Apprenticeships"** for 16 and 17 year olds from 1995. These will offer work-based training to NVQ Level 3. TECs will work with local employers to organise the supply of places. The Government has challenged employers to invest in this important skills area and make training places available. The aim is that by the end of the decade there will be 150,000 new apprentices in training in England at any one time, and over 40,000 young people each year achieving qualifications at NVQ Level 3 or above.

4.31 By 1995, all young school-leavers in England and mainland Scotland will be offered **training credits** at age 16 or 17. These will enable them to obtain YT or Modern Apprenticeships from an employer or other recognised training provider. The experience of the current TEC- and lec-operated pilot schemes is that credits boost the motivation of young people to train, as well as employers' willingness to invest in their training.

Beyond 19

4.32 Higher Education will provide our key managers and professional staff in the decades ahead. There has been record expansion, and record numbers, in British higher education in recent years. In 1979 one young person in eight entered a full-time course; now it is close to one in three (chart 4.7). We have the highest graduation rate in Europe. The next three years will be a period of consolidation, in which universities and colleges can secure and extend their recent improvements in output and efficiency and focus on the maintenance and enhancement of quality. The Government remains committed to a continuing high output of good quality graduates to meet the needs of our society and our economy.

4.33 Universities and colleges are increasingly responding to the need to develop the skills and aptitudes which employers want, such as communication, enterprise and management. The Enterprise in Higher Education initiative has

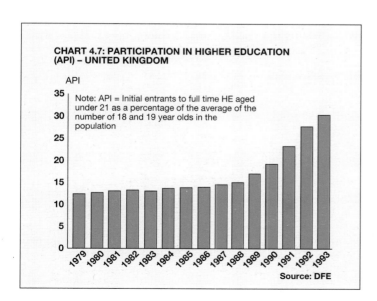

CHART 4.7: PARTICIPATION IN HIGHER EDUCATION (API) – UNITED KINGDOM

API

Note: API = Initial entrants to full time HE aged under 21 as a percentage of the average of the number of 18 and 19 year olds in the population

Source: DFE

brought academics and industrialists together to help students prepare for the work-place. Industrial placements and experience are encouraged, and many academic courses now include teaching in management and business. Many universities help employers establish development programmes for their staff, and are working with TECs and other bodies representing employers' interests.

4.34 A new edition of the Charter for Higher Education, in 1995/6, will set out what students, employers and the local community are entitled to expect from the universities with which they deal.

Lifetime Learning

4.35 Learning does not stop when work starts. For example, 40,000 managers are working towards NVQs. Others are upgrading their skills through short vocational courses provided by universities, colleges and other providers. There is a steady increase in the number of workers taking higher education degrees.

4.36 The Government is continuing to encourage the use of Career Development Loans (CDLs), which enable adults to draw on private sector loan capital to invest more of their own resources in training. There is provision for some 20,000 people to use the scheme in 1994/5. In addition the Government has made tax relief available to individuals who buy training leading to NVQs. The Government is building on the success of the CDL approach by enabling small firms to draw on private sector capital to train their employees.

4.37 Employers have the major role in spreading effective lifetime learning throughout the workforce and in ensuring that it meets business needs and quality standards, for example through using NVQs. In this they have the help of ITOs in their sectors and TECs/lecs locally. Employer interest in getting recognition as **Investors in People** is growing rapidly. The setting up last year of Investors in People UK provides business leadership and oversight at national level for the drive for high quality standards of training and staff development. Action is also being taken to raise the quality of British management training (described in chapter six).

4.38 Following the Government's labour market reforms, employers are able to set pay differentials which better reflect the skills and abilities of individual employees. As well as investing in job-specific skills, some companies give their employees an entitlement to financial support for general education and training in their own time.

EMPLOYERS' ROLE IN LIFETIME LEARNING

Employers:

- *have played a major role in establishing the TEC network two years ahead of schedule. 750 business leaders provide unpaid support as TEC directors*
- *now spend an estimated £20 billion per year on the training and development of their staff. Almost two thirds of employers with 25 or more employees have a training plan for their workforce, and over 50 per cent have established a specific training budget*
- *provided in 1993 job-related training over a period of four weeks or more for 2.8 million employees (an increase of some 70 per cent from 1984). An increasingly high number of establishments provide off the job training (80 per cent in 1993)*
- *are increasingly working towards the Investors in People standard. 6,600 organisations are committed to it and over 800 already meet it*
- *between 1987 and 1993 the number of people on the labour market with a qualification rose by over 2.7 million to 79 per cent. 48 per cent had at least a GCE A level or equivalent*

SCOTLAND

Scotland's distinctive system of education and training promotes rising achievements:

- *74 per cent of pupils **stay on at school** at 16, with 28 per cent (and 35 per cent projected by the year 2000) attaining 3 or more Highers – the threshold for entry to Higher Education*
- *a **new curriculum and assessment programme** is being introduced for 5-14 year olds which aims to improve standards, assessment and reporting to parents. An updated Parent's Charter will be issued later this year*
- *a new unified framework of courses and assessment for upper secondary education has just been announced. Courses will be restructured to raise standards and to promote parity of esteem between academic and vocational subjects*
- *the **Careers Service** is working towards new nationwide standards of provision with a stronger employer focus. Other steps to boost its effectiveness will be considered as part of the Secretary of State for Scotland's new responsibility for training policy*
- *a rise of 13 per cent is projected in the number of **Further Education** college students. A new funding formula will reward efficient expansion*
- *the number of young people participating in **Higher Education** has gone up from 1 in 6 in 1979 to over 1 in 3 in 1992/3. Planned expenditure provides for the participation of over 35 per cent*
- *the number of trainees in **national training programmes** run by lecs enjoying employed status, gaining vocational qualifications and successfully entering employment or further training have all grown since 1991. Scotland has already met Foundation Target 3 of the National Education and Training Targets, with more than 50 per cent of young people achieving at least SVQ level 3 or equivalent, and 40 per cent of young trainees have employed status*
- *over 500 companies in Scotland are committed to becoming **Investors in People**; 70 per cent of these companies are small firms*
- *the Advisory Scottish Council for **Education and Training Targets** recently launched new targets. By the year 2000 85 per cent of young people should attain SVQ level 2 and 70 per cent of young people SVQ level 3; 60 per cent of the workforce should be qualified to at least SVQ level 3 and 50 per cent of organisations be recognised or committed to Investors in People*

WALES

Wales has further to go to meet the National Targets for Education and Training than England, Scotland or Northern Ireland:

- *in November 1993, the Secretary of State for Wales published his consultation document "**People and Prosperity – A Challenge to Wales"** [1]*
- *the document discussed what needs to be done to help the people of Wales develop the skills and initiative to compete with the best in the world*
- *in the light of the responses to the consultation document, the Secretary of State will publish, later this year, guidance setting out how the Government's strategy on education, training and enterprise will be carried forward in ways which reflect the needs of Wales, and which build on the policies set out in this chapter*

NORTHERN IRELAND

The education and training system in Northern Ireland, though different in structure from the rest of the United Kingdom, promotes rising standards:

- *the **Northern Ireland Curriculum** is being introduced for 4-16 years olds. It aims to provide a broad and balanced programme of study. It is supported by a system of assessment which aims to improve standards and reporting to parents. The Department of Education, Northern Ireland (DENI) publishes the examination results of schools annually, and a Northern Ireland Parent's Charter has been issued*
- *in 1992/3, 75 per cent of 16 year olds stayed in full-time education. The proportion of pupils reaching compulsory school leaving age with five or more **GCSEs** at grades A-C has risen to 48 per cent in Northern Ireland in 1993. The proportion of school leavers with two or more GCA **A levels** has risen from 20 per cent in 1986/7 to 30 per cent in 1992/3*
- *the participation rate in **higher education** has reached almost 39 per cent in 1993*
- *the options open to young people remaining at school post-16 have been increased by encouraging schools to make available **vocational qualifications,** particularly GNVQs*
- ***careers** is a cross-curricular theme at secondary level. DENI and the Training and Employment Agency (T&EA) have carried out a review of careers guidance to provide a more effective service*
- *the **T&EA** was set up in 1990 to enhance skills in Northern Ireland*
- *training schemes for young people and the unemployed are being restructured into a new Jobskills programme*

New Initiatives

4.39 The nation's achievements in recent years are striking. But if we are to take full advantage of the opportunities offered by advances in technology and product markets we must do still more. TECs, employers, ITOs, individuals, schools, colleges and other providers all need to play their part in producing the world class workforce. The Government will contribute to this partnership by introducing the following measures and providing resources totalling over £300 million over the next three years to 1997/98.

---

[1] *People and Prosperity - A Challenge to Wales.* [Welsh Office] (1993)

Better Schools

4.40 Following Sir Ron Dearing's reports[2], the **National Curriculum** is being streamlined and testing focused more closely on **key basic skills**. All pupils up to the age of 14 will continue to study the full range of National Curriculum subjects, but priority will be given to the core subjects of English, (and Welsh as a first language in Wales), mathematics and science. This will be backed up by rigorous and challenging tests and an increased emphasis on the basics of literacy and numeracy. Educational standards in Scotland are being tackled through its 5-14 curriculum and assessment programme.

4.41 In addition to continuing to study English, mathematics and science, 14-16 year olds in England will be required to follow at least a short course in a modern foreign language and in technology. These slimmed down requirements mean that there will be greater scope for 14 year olds to opt for **vocational courses**. The School Curriculum and Assessment Authority (SCAA) and NCVQ are working on the development of new vocational qualifications specifically designed for this age group. These will occupy half the time of a full GNVQ and can serve as a basis for further vocational courses post 16. The first of these courses is expected to be piloted in schools in 1995.

4.42 As a spur to improved performance in the key subjects, the Government will introduce in 1995 a **new General Diploma** in England. This will be available to 16 year olds or recent school leavers gaining GCSEs at grades A*-C in English, mathematics and science, plus any other two GCSE subjects at the same level or their vocational equivalents. The diploma will act for employers and others as a clear "quality check", showing that the holder has mastered the basics. In Wales the diploma will reflect the requirement to study Welsh in Welsh-medium schools. In Scotland the new arrangements for upper secondary education will allow students to gain National Certificate group awards at various levels.

4.43 From 1995/6, the Government will introduce a voucher scheme for training newly appointed **headteachers in leadership and management skills** in all maintained schools.

[2] Sir Ron Dearing; *The National Curriculum and its Assessment: interim report* [National Curriculum Council & School Examinations and Assessment Council] (1993) Sir Ron Dearing; *The National Curriculum and its Assessment: final report* [School Curriculum and Assessment Authority] (1994)

16-19: Helping Young Adults to Succeed

4.44 The Government will step up the amount and quality of specialist in-service **training for careers teachers** and supporting materials. Careers education and guidance depends on good cooperation between careers teachers and the independent Careers Service. The Government will issue a policy statement on such cooperation and revise the guidance on **good working practice,** "Working Together"[3]. This will be sent to all secondary schools, colleges of Further Education, and Careers Services.

4.45 The Government will expect all schools to provide policy statements on their **careers education** provision and to **enter into agreements with the local Careers Service on the provision of guidance.** The Parent's Charter will cover this, and schools will be expected to describe their arrangements in prospectuses. The OFSTED inspection programme will monitor schools' performance against defined criteria.

4.46 The independent **careers guidance** given to young people through the Careers Service will receive a major boost. Over the next three years to 1997/98 the Government will be providing £87 million to improve the quality and coverage of careers guidance for pupils from age 13. Together with improvements already announced in connection with Modern Apprenticeships, this will nearly double careers guidance provision to young people in schools and colleges by 1997/98. This will bring about a step change in the help young people and their parents receive to make the most appropriate choices.

ENTITLEMENT TO CAREERS EDUCATION AND GUIDANCE

Age 11-16:	*Schools will provide a planned programme of education on post-16 education and training options, and on different types of jobs. Schools will be expected to set out those arrangements in their prospectus*
Age 13-14:	*Careers officers will provide guidance at 14 to all pupils on GCSE choices and vocational options, and where they can lead*
Age 15-16:	*Careers Officers will conduct an individual interview with each pupil on post-16 choices, with inputs from teachers and school records. Parents will be invited to attend and will receive a copy of the report and action plan afterwards*
Age 17-18:	*Every young person remaining in full-time education will be offered further information and guidance by the Careers Service on post-18 choices*

---

[3] *Working Together for a Better Future.* [Department of Education and Science, Employment Department, Welsh Office] (1987)

4.47 Careers education in Scotland is provided as part of Scotland's distinctive guidance arrangements for secondary schools. Comparable steps to enter agreements with the Careers Service and set out pupils entitlement will be taken. The Government will consider the case for further careers, education and guidance measures in Scotland, tailored to its particular education and training system.

A better introduction to the world of work

4.48 The Government will increase the resources for spreading best practice identified through TVEI, so that the key results of the initiative are fully embedded in the work of every school. TECs have stimulated a network of local partnerships to co-ordinate links between education and business. The Government will ask TECs and their partners to ensure that all pupils in their last year of compulsory education can have at least one week's work experience, and will make available funding, amounting to £23 million over the three years to 1997/98, to support this. The Government will also encourage improved focus and quality in school-business links by asking TECs and their partners to work towards the objectives set out in the Box.

OBJECTIVES FOR SCHOOL-BUSINESS LINKS

The Government hopes Education-Business Partnerships will:

- *offer every young person at least one week of work experience in their last year of compulsory education and a further week for those aged 16-18 who stay on in full time education*
- *enable, every year, 10 per cent of primary and secondary school teachers, with a particular focus on headteachers, to receive a suitable placement in business and that every year each school receives a placement from business*
- *encourage every employer with more than 200 employees, every year, to release at least one employee for a week's placement in a school*
- *encourage employer endorsement of pupils' work experience in the National Record of Achievement and encourage use of the Record in employee recruitment*

Better qualifications

4.49 GCE A level and AS qualifications will be strengthened further. To help ensure consistent high standards of assessment in GCE Examinations, the examining boards will introduce **a common Code of Practice** in time for the 1994 examinations. The Government is considering steps to recognise exceptional achievement, and inviting SCAA and other interested parties to take action to make **AS courses more attractive to young people**. More generally, the Government will encourage syllabuses with a greater emphasis on practical application.

4.50 The Government is determined that **GNVQs will be rigorous and consistent.** It is therefore asking NCVQ to:

- review the assessment and grading system;

- clarify the knowledge required;

- work closely with SCAA on matters of mutual interest; and

- ensure better links between general and occupation-specific vocational qualifications.

4.51 Work will continue to ensure the successful introduction of GNVQs – including Advanced GNVQs, the new vocational A levels – in schools and colleges, including through **teacher training.**

4.52 The Government will also ensure that NVQs and SVQs remain up to date and continue to observe strict standards. **The content and structure of all existing NVQs and SVQs will be reviewed by April 1996.** The 100 most frequently used qualifications will be covered by December 1995. Local and national promotion to employers will be improved and local quality assurance arrangements developed.

Better choice and responsiveness

4.53 The Government will act to secure still **closer cooperation between the FEFC, colleges and TECs** at national, regional and local level. Colleges will work more closely with TECs on the preparation of college strategic plans to ensure they are closely adapted to local labour market needs, and these plans will be subject to TEC approval. This means that the TEC influence will be integrated into mainstream funding. As a result funding arrangements will change. At present a proportion of funding for colleges in England is routed through TECs. Most of that funding will be re-routed through FEFC but a proportion will continue to be used by TECs for development purposes. In addition, a new **Competitiveness Fund** will be established, to be administered by TECs. This will help colleges meet particularly critical labour market needs, including the purchase of state of the art capital equipment and related items for use in these areas. The Secretary of State for Wales will announce arrangements in Wales in due course.

4.54 The Government is establishing a **new body to promote quality in the FE sector,** with a major role in improving management training and development for college staff.

4.55 The Government has already challenged employers to establish Modern Apprenticeships for 16-17 year olds. Of course, many young people stay at school or college until 18. The Government wants these young people also to have the opportunity of a first class modern apprenticeship to get proper work based skills and qualifications. The Government will challenge industry to develop, from 1995,

accelerated Modern Apprenticeships for 18-19 year olds. As with Modern Apprenticeships, accelerated Modern Apprenticeships will be a partnership between ITOs and TECs. If industry plays its part, Government will provide funding of £107 million over the three years to 1997/98. This means that by the end of the century an extra 30,000 young people a year will achieve NVQs at Level 3 or higher. This will make a major contribution to skill supply.

4.56 The quality and relevance of the learning secured by our young people as they make the transition from school to work are of special importance to our long term competitiveness. Young people need to learn how to take responsibility for their own decisions, and to appreciate the crucial importance of investing in skills. At the same time the providers of training and education should be responsive to their customers. The Government therefore sees attractions in providing all 16-19 year olds with **learning credits,** with a real cash value.

4.57 Learning credits would give young people the power to buy their own education and training from schools, colleges, employers and other recognised providers. They have been advocated by the CBI and others, and would fit well with the Government's overall policy of promoting choice and diversity. They could build on the experience of training credits, currently operated by TECs.

4.58 The Government recognises that such a far-reaching change in funding would need careful preparation. The Government therefore intends to consult further on the practical implications of learning credits, and to discuss the issues widely and openly. In the light of these consultations it will consider introducing pilot schemes based on local partnerships, to provide more information and experience before final decisions are taken at a later stage.

Lifetime Learning

4.59 Improved education and training for children and young adults will help all employers and their current and future employees. But **small firms** can face particular difficulties in providing modern skills training for their employees, especially where substantial off the job training is involved. The Government will:

- make available funding totalling £63 million over the three years to 1997/98 to update the managerial, supervisory and technical skills of up to 24,000 key employees in firms with fewer than 50 employees. This funding will help trained people share their skills with others. These "mentors" can then train and assess staff in their own and other small firms;

- encourage TECs to work with Business Links and other networks serving small firms, so that such companies are able to work together to find shared, cost effective ways to meet training needs;

- encourage TECs to ask large firms which have already been recognised as Investors in People to offer training advisors to small supplier firms to help them introduce NVQs and Investors in People; and

- operate these measures alongside the new small firms training loans which will already help up to 30,000 individuals in 1997/98.

4.60 The Government will be taking a number of steps to **encourage the spread of the Investors in People initiative**. In particular, additional resources will allow promotion of the initiative to be stepped up. To improve staff development of their civil servants and secure best value for money from their investment in training, more Government departments are already committing themselves to work towards the Investors in People standard. All other Government departments will now carry forward their plans to become Investors in People.

4.61 The Government will also encourage improved **vocational information and advice for adults,** through such means as TEC-managed advice points and other local advisory services.

4.62 The Government will help individuals assume greater responsibility for their own development and training throughout their life, and support their willingness to invest in it personally. To this end, the Government will seek ways to make the CDL Scheme more accessible to clients changing or seeking jobs. There may also be attractions in **voluntary individual training accounts.** Such arrangements could, for example, enable individuals to save money in a commercial or employer-based fund, which could be topped up by contributions from employers, TECs and others. The Government will consult TECs, financial institutions and other bodies on how to take forward such arrangements in the most effective way.

Europe

4.63 The Government will assist education and training providers to rise to the challenges of the Single Market. It will play a full part in promoting the dissemination of educational expertise through EC Programmes. These offer opportunities for providers of vocational education and training to exchange successful practice, and so capitalise on innovation and policy development across Member States. The Government will also continue to press for these programmes, and the operation of such funding mechanisms as the European Social Fund, to be geared to increasing the competitiveness of Europe and its enterprises.

Conclusions

4.64 The Government's commitment to securing higher achievement throughout the education and training system is clear. It has set a framework within which employers, schools, colleges and other training providers, together with TECs and lecs, are delivering improving results. Participation and achievement are at record levels. But we need to match the speed of change of our competitors abroad. The drive towards continuous improvement must be sustained and quickened.

4.65 This chapter has set out a demanding and radical package of reforms which will secure emerging success and help the drive forward. The thrust of the reforms will be to integrate our education and training efforts more effectively whilst extending diversity and choice, and ensuring flexibility and the capacity for further improvement by ambitious individuals and institutions. The key new engines of change are:

- a streamlined and rigorous National Curriculum with more emphasis on the basics – English, mathematics and science;

- more opportunities for vocational study for 14-16 year olds;

- better careers education and guidance to help young people choose the best path to their future;

- a demanding and popular range of academic and vocational qualifications at 16 and beyond;

- a new framework of objectives for education-business links at local level with funding to support the objective that all 14-15 year olds should have a week's work experience;

- new accelerated apprenticeships for England and Wales offering 18 and 19 year olds high level work-based qualifications (the Secretary of State for Scotland is also considering this and other options in his review of training strategy in Scotland);

- new help for small firms to train trainers and mentors who will in turn train other employees;

- a further boost to Investors in People;

- further support for individuals wishing to commit to lifetime learning; and

- greater responsiveness by providers to the needs of their customers – learners and employers – including closer examination of the learning credits approach to education and training.

EMPLOYMENT

5.1 Flexible labour markets play a key part in a competitive economy. They allow employers to deploy their workforce in the most efficient way. They allow workers to make the most of their skills and experience. And they bring supply and demand for labour into balance.

5.2 An efficient labour market is one in which:

- employment and labour productivity are maximised by efficient matching of supply and demand;

- wages are based on local labour market conditions;

- enterprises are characterised by responsive management, good industrial relations and flexible bargaining systems; and

- freedom from discrimination and rigid workplace demarcations allows individuals to make their full economic contribution.

5.3 An economy underpinned by these strengths can grow at a faster sustainable rate. Output is higher, employment grows, skills are rewarded and living standards rise. Tackling inefficiencies in the labour market has a crucial part to play in reducing unemployment.

5.4 Government, employers and employees all have a part to play. We need to create a series of virtuous circles in which high quality basic education creates the foundation for training throughout working life; in which good employee relations, employee involvement and flexible working patterns lead to job satisfaction, higher productivity, increased profitability and increased employment; and in which the absence of discrimination leads to everyone realising their full potential.

The problem

5.5 In the 1960s and 1970s the problems were plain for all to see:

- wage rises failing to reflect performance, affordability and recruitment and retention needs;

- firms' unit labour costs rising faster than those in other countries, expressed in national currencies (chart 5.1);

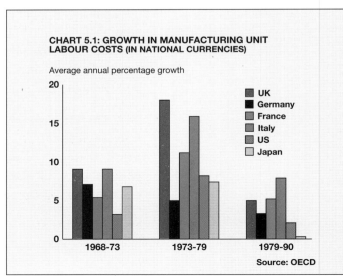

CHART 5.1: GROWTH IN MANUFACTURING UNIT LABOUR COSTS (IN NATIONAL CURRENCIES)

Average annual percentage growth

Legend: UK, Germany, France, Italy, US, Japan

Source: OECD

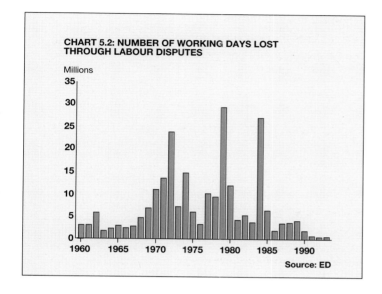

CHART 5.2: NUMBER OF WORKING DAYS LOST THROUGH LABOUR DISPUTES

Millions

Source: ED

- as rising costs fed inflation, firms mistakenly believing that exchange rate depreciation would maintain their competitiveness;

- poor industrial relations;

- high levels of industrial disruption (chart 5.2);

- high unemployment and job vacancies increasingly existing side by side; and

- each successive trough in the economic cycle generating ever higher levels of unemployment.

The Government's approach

5.6 Since 1979, the Government has followed a wide-ranging strategy aimed at improving the working of the labour market. The main objectives are:

- **to encourage good employment practices.** Successful firms encourage genuine dialogue between managers and workers, and secure commitment and high performance through quality training, good working conditions, and rewards which fairly reflect individual performance, the local labour market and the circumstances of the firm. This has been a key feature of Japanese success. The Government has introduced tax reliefs to encourage financial participation by employees, and promoted good practice in employee involvement generally;

- **to improve industrial relations.** The Government has outlawed closed shop practices, flying pickets and calls for secondary action, and given businesses more protection against unofficial action;

- **to maintain a fair framework of individual employment rights, while minimising costs to employers.** The Government has sought to strike the right balance by guaranteeing minimum standards, and providing effective arrangements for redress and enforcement, whilst reviewing existing requirements, pressing the European Commission for proper assessment of the effects of their proposals, and reducing legislative burdens, particularly on the smallest firms;

- **to reform and encourage change in wage bargaining arrangements.** The Government has taken steps to enable settlements to be more responsive to the performance of firms and individuals and to local labour markets. The Dock Labour Scheme and the Wages Council system for setting and enforcing statutory minimum wage rates have been abolished;

ABOLITION OF DOCK LABOUR SCHEME

Since abolition, industrial disputes have been dramatically reduced:
- *in 1988, the last full year of the Scheme, over 10,000 man days were lost in industrial action in Scheme ports*
- *in 1991 only one ex-Scheme port experienced strike action, resulting in 500 man days lost*

and productivity greatly increased:
- *in 1988, 492 million tonnes were handled by 17,500 dock workers*
- *in 1991, 495 million tonnes were handled by 12,000 dock workers*

- **to maximise the effective supply of labour and competition for jobs.** The number of people who are competing for jobs and the intensity of their job search influences labour costs. Weak labour supply leads to inflation rather than more jobs when output grows. The Government has enhanced incentives to work, provided information and active help for unemployed people, discouraged unfair discrimination in the labour market, and removed obstacles to labour mobility; and

- **to enhance the quality of our work force,** as described in the previous chapter.

INCENTIVES TO WORK

The Government aims to ensure that people are encouraged to take work. Activity should be rewarded more generously than inactivity. Systems need to be administered efficiently, so that people can be confident of receiving the in-work benefits to which they are entitled.

The Government has:
- *reduced the basic rate of income tax from 33 to 25 per cent*
- *introduced a 20 per cent tax band for the first £3000 of taxable income*
- *reformed social security benefits to improve incentives to work*
- *extended Family Credit to those working 16 hours a week or more: one third of Family Credit recipients are now working between 16 and 24 hours a week*
- *introduced a "fast-track" system for Family Credit to ensure that those moving from unemployment into employment do not have long waits for payment*
- *introduced Disability Working Allowance, to provide a new opportunity for disabled people to work*
- *significantly improved publicity and information for unemployed people about in-work benefits*

MOBILITY OF LABOUR

One way of avoiding shortages of labour and skills is to minimise obstacles which prevent people moving to take up the most suitable job.

The Government has:

- *pursued policies to expand home ownership. The market in private housing is responsive to changes in the pattern of labour demand. 67 per cent of English households are now home-owners, compared to 57 per cent in 1979*
- *stimulated growth in the private rented sector to increase choice for those who want to rent when they move. There are now 1.9 million English households in this sector, compared to 1.7 million in 1988*
- *substantially improved the position of early leavers in occupational pension schemes and introduced transfer rights for those changing jobs*
- *introduced greater choice and flexibility to encourage personal pension provision*

The UK Labour Market Today

5.7 The Government's labour market reforms have been far-reaching and influential.

5.8 The climate of industrial relations has dramatically improved. The UK's record and reputation have been transformed:

- in 1993 only 0.6 million working days were lost because of industrial disputes, less than 2 per cent of the 1979 figure and well below even the 1980s average of 7.2 million days lost per year; and

- the UK strike rate is now well below the EC and OECD average level and, in recent years, that in the US (chart 5.3).

5.9 Employers have encouraged greater employee involvement. They have also introduced more responsive bargaining arrangements:

- the joint CBI and Employment Department programme "Managing for Success" is raising awareness of the benefits of employee involvement;

- there is some form of employee involvement in over 90 per cent of all workplaces;

- the number of national multi-employer collective agreements fell sharply between 1984 and 1990; and

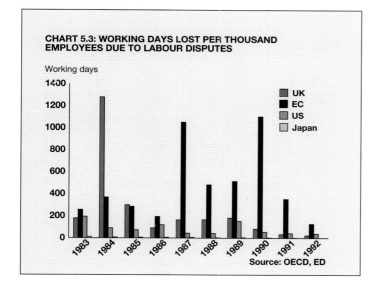

CHART 5.3: WORKING DAYS LOST PER THOUSAND EMPLOYEES DUE TO LABOUR DISPUTES

Working days

Legend: UK, EC, US, Japan

Source: OECD, ED

- new forms of payment system are spreading: 74 per cent of employers now use some form of performance related pay.

EXAMPLES OF BENEFITS ACHIEVED THROUGH EMPLOYEE INVOLVEMENT

- *The introduction of teamworking has produced annual cost savings of nearly £2 million in an electrical goods factory and has helped to increase profits despite a fall in sales*
- *The establishment of self-managed teams has helped a factory in the automotive component industry to achieve an increase in productivity of nearly 30 per cent and a 16 per cent reduction in process and material costs*
- *A performance appraisal system in a retail and servicing outlet has resulted in a reduction of staff turnover from 15 to 3 per cent and has produced customer satisfaction levels of 90 per cent*
- *An employee buyout in a bus company has resulted in a doubling of company profits and an increase in the ordinary share value of over 500 per cent*

5.10 These changes are beginning to produce more responsive earnings, higher productivity and lower unit wage costs. They have also had an important impact on unemployment rates and jobs growth.

5.11 During the 1980s, earnings grew faster than was justified by improved performance. More recently, average earnings have been growing much more slowly. Our hourly labour costs in manufacturing remain below those of the other G7 nations, as they have done for at least the last five years. Our low non-wage costs are a major factor in this, and give us a significant competitive advantage (chart 5.4). There has also been an increase in pay differentials for skills. This should have a beneficial effect on incentives to train, building on the training reforms described in the previous chapter.

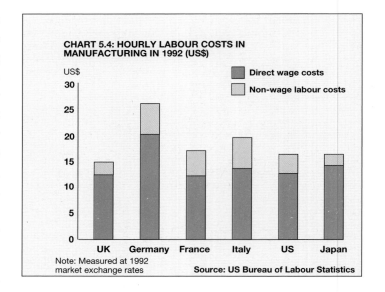

CHART 5.4: HOURLY LABOUR COSTS IN MANUFACTURING IN 1992 (US$)

Direct wage costs
Non-wage labour costs

Note: Measured at 1992 market exchange rates

Source: US Bureau of Labour Statistics

5.12 The 1980s saw a transformation of the UK's manufacturing productivity performance. The combination of slower earnings increases and rising productivity has slowed the growth in unit wage costs. 1993 saw the smallest rise in unit wage costs since the series began in 1970.

EXAMPLES OF FLEXIBLE WORKING PATTERNS

- *Nearly two million employees now work under an annual hours system. Employees' hours are arranged on a yearly rather than weekly basis, allowing greater flexibility for them and for employers*
- *Many companies make use of "teleworking" arrangements, where staff work at home using computers and telecommunications technology. This has helped to reduce costs for employers and employees, increase productivity and retain skilled staff*
- *Around 250,000 employees now work on a job-share basis*
- *Employers in seasonal industries (for example agriculture and travel) have increasingly introduced new shiftwork patterns to ensure extra staff resources are available during peak months*
- *Unions in the motor industry have accepted more flexible working arrangements, including the elimination of demarcation*

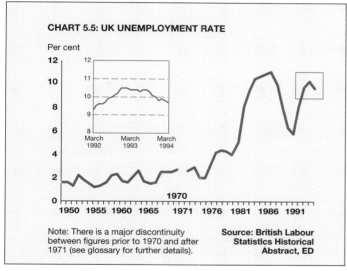

CHART 5.5: UK UNEMPLOYMENT RATE

Per cent

Note: There is a major discontinuity between figures prior to 1970 and after 1971 (see glossary for further details).

Source: British Labour Statistics Historical Abstract, ED

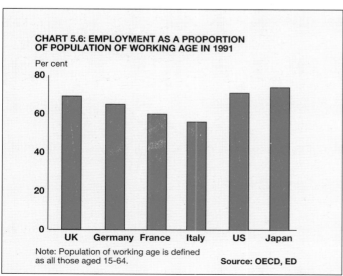

CHART 5.6: EMPLOYMENT AS A PROPORTION OF POPULATION OF WORKING AGE IN 1991

Per cent

Note: Population of working age is defined as all those aged 15-64.

Source: OECD, ED

5.13 Unemployment remains uncomfortably high (chart 5.5), as it has done in many of the G7 countries since the early 1980s. But recent signs are encouraging:

- during the last economic cycle, employment grew by 1.3 million – the best performance during an economic cycle since 1960;

- the UK labour market sustains higher employment rates than any other EC country except Denmark and Portugal (chart 5.6), and a wide variety of working patterns, reflecting the needs of companies and individuals alike for greater flexibility;

- unemployment began to fall at an earlier stage in the current recovery, and its peak level was below the peak in the previous economic cycle for the first time since the 1960s;

- long-term (over 12 months) unemployment as a proportion of total unemployment – currently 37 per cent – is much lower than the previous peak in 1987. On the most recent available comparison, the UK position is better than that of other major EC countries, (chart 5.7);

• there has been a significant decrease in the ratio of unemployed people to vacancies;

• regional disparities in unemployment have narrowed significantly. Scotland, traditionally a high unemployment area, now has a rate below the national average; and

• around two thirds of people who become unemployed leave the unemployment register within six months.

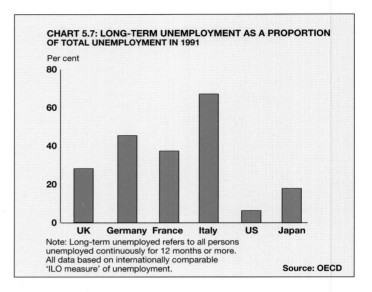

CHART 5.7: LONG-TERM UNEMPLOYMENT AS A PROPORTION OF TOTAL UNEMPLOYMENT IN 1991

Per cent

Note: Long-term unemployed refers to all persons unemployed continuously for 12 months or more. All data based on internationally comparable 'ILO measure' of unemployment.

Source: OECD

ACTIVE HELP TO GET UNEMPLOYED PEOPLE INTO WORK

A flexible labour market needs active measures to help unemployed people back into work – especially for the long-term unemployed who find getting back to work most difficult. The administration of benefits needs to ensure that unemployed people look actively for work and take advantage of the available opportunities. The Government has:

• *brought together Unemployment Benefit Offices and Jobcentres within the Employment Service to emphasise the link between receiving benefit and job search*

• *developed a range of measures to help unemployed people back to work:*
  • *access to a wide range of job vacancies*
  • *back-to-work counselling and advice*
  • *help with looking for work and restoring motivation*
  • *encouragement for employers to recruit long-term unemployed people*
  • *access to training*

  providing 1½ million opportunities this year

• *significantly increased the Employment Service's target for placing long-term claimants into jobs – to ½ million in 1994/95*

• *placed requirements on people who receive unemployment and related benefits:*
  • *to be available for work*
  • *to seek work actively*
  • *to seek work widely and be prepared to accept any job after a period of more restricted job search*
  • *to attend six-monthly interviews to review their job search activity and receive offers of help*
  • *to respond positively when directed towards suitable employment opportunities*
  • *to attend a Jobplan Workshop or Restart Course when they pass the twelve or twenty-four month thresholds of unemployment and turn down all other offers of help*

• *made those who claim unemployment related benefits aware that failure to comply with these requirements could result in loss or reduction of benefits*

ACTIVE LABOUR POLICIES IN OTHER COUNTRIES
United States

US Government intervention in the labour market is limited. Compared to most European countries, coverage of unemployment insurance is narrow; maximum levels of benefit and ratios of benefits to income in work are low; and the duration of benefit payment is short. There are strict eligibility requirements for benefits.

Federal expenditure on active labour market measures such as job training has been low compared to other OECD countries. However it has recently been given a higher priority with the development of retraining for unemployed people within the Workforce Investment Strategy. Some States operate limited "workfare" schemes.

Sweden

The Swedish approach has two elements. Much weight is initially given to placing unemployed people into jobs, with subsequent extensive employment and training programmes. These are designed to keep unemployed people in touch with the labour market by maintaining their work habits and skills. Labour market programmes are directly counter-cyclical. In 1993, with unemployment at a record high, 5.5 per cent of the labour force was involved in Government-funded job-creation measures.

Direct unemployment benefit has a maximum initial duration of 14 months, but when combined with guaranteed periods on training or employment programmes it can be unlimited. Failure to participate in these programmes can result in benefit sanctions. There are places on them in both the public and private sectors. The programmes are expensive; in 1990 expenditure on active labour market measures represented 1.6 per cent of GDP. They cannot on their own solve unemployment. The Government has more recently introduced cheaper programmes which pay less to participants.

New Initiatives

5.14 The Government is determined to build on the success of its reforms. Future plans focus on further strengthening individual rights and responsibilities; and extending choice, flexibility and opportunity.

5.15 The last 15 years have demonstrated that modernisation and reform of **industrial relations and trade union** law can contribute significantly to helping promote good industrial relations, more effective management, and higher productivity. The Government will continue to keep the legal framework under review.

5.16 The Government looks to employers and their workforces to continue to take full advantage of the more flexible framework which now governs relations at work. There are encouraging signs that managers and workers are increasingly co-operating to help companies improve competitiveness and adapt to change.

5.17 The Government will continue to promote effective **employee involvement.** Such arrangements must be flexible. Attempts to impose a single regulatory framework, such as the European Commission's proposal for a directive on informing and consulting employees in transnational companies, fail to take account of real business needs in a competitive environment. The Government will ensure that such constraints are not imposed in the UK.

5.18 The Government welcomes action by companies, employers' organisations, and other industry bodies to promote effective involvement of employees and the sharing of experience. It is publishing a booklet, "The Competitive Edge"[1], which surveys different ways of informing, consulting and otherwise involving the workforce. The booklet is illustrated by good practice drawn from a wide range of successful organisations, and will be distributed to employers' organisations, trade associations and trade unions.

5.19 The Government will continue to ensure that the scope and form of **employment rights for individuals** strike a proper balance with the potential burdens to employers and the economy. Proposals from Europe will be carefully scrutinised. Deregulatory measures will be introduced where the opportunity offers.

5.20 The Government will continue to promote an effective system of health and safety regulation which, while maintaining proper standards, does not impose unnecessary burdens. It has examined the scope for removing outdated regulations and eliminating unnecessary bureaucracy, in the light of recommendations from the Health and Safety Commission. Details are set out in chapter 13.

5.21 The Government is seeking to develop and strengthen its **active labour market policies:** first, using existing legislation to require more activity by people who are unemployed; and second, through the new Jobseeker's Allowance.

5.22 It has continued to develop measures to ensure that people take advantage of the opportunities available to them, and take active steps to get back to work. A New Restart Course and two experimental pilots began in April:

- New Restart Courses: a two week course for those who have been unemployed for two years or more which will combine part-time attendance at formal sessions with agreed and recorded job search activity;

- Workwise Course: a pilot four-week assessment and job search course for people in the 18-24 age range who have been unemployed for at least a year; and

- 1-2-1 Interviews: another pilot for 18-24 year olds who have been unemployed for over a year, which will assign participants to an individual caseworker for a series of up to six counselling and job search interviews.

In each case, people in the target group will be required to attend, and will face a benefit sanction if they fail to do so.

---

[1] *The Competitive Edge* [Employment Department] (1994)

5.23 The Jobseeker's Allowance will be introduced in 1996 to replace Income Support for unemployed people and Unemployment Benefit. It will emphasise the responsibilities of unemployed people who are paid unemployment benefits, whilst at the same time offering improved help to get back to work as quickly as possible:

- claimants will complete a Jobseeker's Agreement which will help them to identify from the outset the steps they will take to get back to work. There will be regular reviews to establish the steps which claimants have taken to find employment, and to offer advice on job search;

- there will be financial penalties for those who are not making substantial efforts to find work;

- there will be one set of rules to replace the overlapping rules of the two existing benefits; and

- Jobseekers will be told clearly the standards and services they can expect and what is expected of them in return.

5.24 The Government's reforms have alleviated the unemployment trap: there is now only a small number of people in work who would receive more in Income Support than they get in wages. The Government is keen to increase **incentives to work**, particularly for those who have been unemployed for a long time.

5.25 The Government will continue to look for ways to encourage employers to recruit long-term unemployed people, and is piloting new initiatives. Some long-term unemployed people can face a financial disincentive to take up work because they lack the resources to meet essential costs such as clothes or transport, or because they have accumulated debts. The Government is therefore piloting a Jobfinder's Grant in the Midlands which offers people a one-off payment when they find a job after two years or more unemployment.

5.26 The Government plans to improve incentives for people with families to take up a job, by removing a major stumbling block from the existing social security system. From October 1994 the costs of childcare up to £40 a week will be disregarded when calculating the in-work benefits for families with children. This will help 100,000 people on low earnings and assist a further 50,000 to move off Income Support and into work. In April the Family Credit claims process for unemployed people who want to become self-employed was simplified, and a new fast track claims system set up for them.

5.27 Unfair discrimination in the labour market is morally wrong and economically damaging. The Government is taking further steps to discourage unfair discrimination. Building on the Chwarae Teg Initiative in Wales, the Government recently launched a new initiative, "Fair Play for Women". This describes the range of Government activities to help women, and introduces new regional partnerships. These bring together groups of decision makers in each English region to help women reach their full potential. This complements the New Horizons campaign to promote women's opportunities. A similar initiative is planned for Northern Ireland and is being considered for Scotland. The Government is expanding the out-of-school childcare initiative to over 20,000 places in 1994/95.

5.28 It is a priority for the Employment Service to help people who have been out of work for a long time or have other disadvantages. The Government will also take further steps to stimulate action by employers. This will include guidance on setting up and developing equal opportunity groups.

5.29 The Government has supported a Private Member's Bill, introduced by Keith Vaz MP, which aims to remove the ceiling on compensation awards for racial discrimination cases in industrial tribunals. The Bill, which has broad cross-party support, has completed all its Parliamentary stages and should become law by the summer. The Government is bringing forward legislation in Northern Ireland to achieve the same change in its fair employment legislation.

5.30 Tackling discrimination and creating more opportunities for disabled people is a priority. Through a continuing programme of education and persuasion, backed up by practical help, and legislation which does not place unreasonable burdens on business, the Government aims to ensure that disabled people have the opportunity to utilise fully their skills and achieve their potential. A number of steps has been taken to educate and persuade employers to think and act positively. These include promoting the "Code of Good Practice on the Employment of Disabled People" and the disability symbol. Practical help to overcome barriers to work is also available, including the Disability Working Allowance benefit. The introduction of Access to Work on 6 June 1994 will make available a wider range of help to more people. Access to Work replaces and adds to current schemes providing special aids, premises adaptations, reader support for blind people and fares to work. In 1994/95 the budget for the special schemes and Access to Work will be over £14½ million.

5.31 Action on pensions and housing will aid **mobility of labour.**

5.32 A discussion document on a new system of age-related rebates for personal pension holders and, possibly, other contracted out pension schemes, was issued in December 1993. The aim is to ensure that personal pensions remain attractive alternatives to the state scheme throughout working lives.

5.33 The Government is also considering the report[2] of the Pensions Law Review Committee, which included a number of recommendations on the transfer of rights from and between occupational pension schemes. These are aimed at smoothing transferability between schemes and underpinning transfer values. A White Paper will be published shortly.

5.34 The Government will continue to encourage the revival of private rented housing. The Department of the Environment and the Welsh Office have consulted on proposals to secure fairer access to local authority and housing association housing and will make announcements on the outcome in due course. A similar consultation will be carried out in Scotland.

[2] *Pension Law Reform: The Report of the Pensions Law Review Committee* Cm2342 I & II [HMSO] (1993)

MANAGEMENT

6.1 While improvements in performance require the efforts of everyone in a company, the contribution of managers is a key element in success. Management is not confined to those at the top of a company – it involves people at all levels, concerned with all aspects of the company's people, processes, products and services.

6.2 High quality management is needed in both the public and private sectors. Both have access to limited resources. Both need to set clear objectives to achieve customer satisfaction. Management in the public sector is covered in the Business of Government chapter. This chapter focuses on management in companies and other private sector bodies – what they can do, and how the Government can help by working in partnership with them.

6.3 By any standards, the management of some UK companies equals or exceeds that of its international competitors:

- three of the top five drinks companies in the world are British;

- a UK company has over one third of the world market for medical and research superconducting magnets;

- a UK manufacturer of probe systems for measuring machines is an acknowledged world leader, exporting 90 per cent of turnover; and

- a micro electronics component and telecommunications systems manufacturer in the UK exports three quarters of its component output to the US and Japan.

6.4 But overall national performance is determined not by the standard of the best but by the average. It is here that the UK lags behind the competition.

The Challenge to Companies

6.5 Successful companies are led by people with a clear vision of the company's objectives and how these are to be achieved, who recognise the need to change and innovate. This is essential for large and small companies alike.

COMPARATIVE DATA ON MANAGEMENT

The CBI[1] has stated that UK manufacturing needs to improve performance by 20-40 per cent to achieve world class standards. Key factors included productivity, stock turn and investment in capital, skills and innovation.

A 1993 study[2] of over 200 UK manufacturing sites showed that:

- *2 per cent had world class manufacturing practices and performance and another 42 per cent were close to world class – but 73 per cent believed that they fully or mostly matched their international competitors*
- *good practices (such as quality management and lean production) do lead to higher performance*
- *leading performers were eight times more likely to base improvements on external benchmarks than the poorest*

An attitude survey[3] in 1993 of over 1,000 managers in Europe's smaller companies (under 500 employees) found that:

- *UK managers thought they were the best in Europe and their companies second only to Germany. Other countries disagreed, placing both UK managers and companies third out of five*
- *this "perception gap" was greater for UK managers than for any others*

6.6 The Royal Society of Arts is working with 25 of the UK's top businesses on an inquiry into "Tomorrow's Company".

6.7 The Government welcomes the inquiry's interim conclusions. They are consistent with those underlying the innovation and best practice work of the Government and CBI.

6.8 Despite the title "Tomorrow's Company", the UK's more successful companies are already implementing many of the recommendations. They demonstrate the

"TOMORROW'S COMPANY"

The conclusions of the inquiry[4] so far are that to achieve sustainable business success in the demanding world marketplace, a company must:

- *be clear about its purpose and values*
- *meet – and exceed – customer demands*
- *learn fast and change fast*
- *inspire its people to new levels of skill, efficiency and creativity*
- *create a sense of shared destiny with all stakeholders (customers, suppliers, employees, investors and the community)*
- *recognise that an exclusive concentration on any one stakeholder will not lead to sustainable competitive performance*
- *use relevant performance measures*

[1] *Making it in Britain II.* [CBI] (1993)

[2] *Made in Britain: the true state of Britain's manufacturing industry.* [IBM Consulting Group and London Business School] (1993)

[3] *Attitudes to Managers and Companies in Europe.* [3i and Cranfield European Enterprise Centre] (1993)

[4] *Tomorrow's Company: The Role of Business in a Changing World.* [Royal Society of Arts] (1994)

importance of innovation and quality as competitive weapons and continually improve their processes, products and services. The challenge for others is to follow suit.

The Government's Contribution

6.9 Responsibility for improving management performance lies with companies. But Government can help them in this process: from helping them to recognise the need for change to assisting with practical implementation. In particular, the Government can:

- identify and disseminate best management practice, and encourage information sharing and cross fertilisation;

- encourage companies to improve management's skill base; and

- provide effective access to a wide range of business services.

Best practice

6.10 There are national, regional and local activities to encourage best practice.

BEST PRACTICE ACTIVITIES: NATIONAL, REGIONAL AND LOCAL EXAMPLES

- *DTI's "Managing in the '90s" programme promotes management best practice in innovation, design, quality, manufacturing and production, purchasing and supply, and marketing. Within that, the "Inside UK Enterprise" scheme offers opportunities to visit and learn from successful UK companies who demonstrate best practice. There are equivalent schemes in Scotland, Wales and in various English regions*
- *CBI's "Competitiveness Forum" brings together senior managers from companies to learn from each other in company visits, seminars and workshops*
- *The British Standards Institution (BSI) works with industry to create standards which encourage best practice. Examples are BS5750, the standard for quality management systems, and BS7750, a new standard on environmental management best practice. Guidance to be issued by DTI will help small businesses seeking BS5750 certification*
- *The National Training Awards attract over 1000 entries annually and encourage best practice in training and development*
- *The Design Council will now concentrate on providing strategic advice, awareness and promotion at the national level. It will also encourage design expertise to be made available to companies locally through Business Links and, in Scotland, Scottish Design*
- *"Manufacturing Challenge" expresses the aim of industry in the North East to double output and treble exports over the decade. It is building a comprehensive network of business to business self help, backed by the Government Office for the North East, the five North East TECs and other business support agencies, to maximise opportunities for growth and develop new strategies*
- *Increasingly, national initiatives are being delivered locally through TECs, lecs and Business Links. Many individual TECs and groups of TECs are active in encouraging local companies to adopt best practice. The "World Class Manufacturing" programmes by TECs in the Midlands and Northern England provide best practice workshops and consultancy*

6.11 To complement these initiatives, the Government is also working with industry through the sponsor divisions in various departments.

BEST PRACTICE ACTIVITIES: SECTORAL EXAMPLES

- *DTI's Benchmarking Challenge encouraged Trade Associations to set up benchmarking clubs to compare current practice, identify best practice and seek improvements. The 13 winners of the competition cover a wide range of sectors. Of those who were not successful, a growing number has decided to go ahead with benchmarking*
- *In the automotive sector, DTI and the Society of Motor Manufacturers & Traders are working with component suppliers to highlight strategic changes and spread best practice down the supply chain. Similar support is provided through the Source Wales initiative*
- *In the forging industry, DTI and Trade Associations have started self help groups to benchmark the sector against the world's best and identify action to improve competitiveness*
- *In construction, DOE is supporting the Construction Quality Forum to create a national database. This will allow building owners, designers and builders to share information on problems and solutions and thus improve quality*
- *The UK Offshore Operators Association and DTI are working with companies to cut capital costs on the UK continental shelf by 30 per cent in 2-3 years*
- *MAFF and the Institute of Grocery Distribution are developing a trading code to help small agricultural and food suppliers deal direct with large buyers*
- *In textiles, DTI and trade associations are promoting the benefits of closer partnerships between retailers and UK manufacturers*
- *In the medical equipment sector, the Welsh Medical Technology Forum is demonstrating the benefits to companies of all sizes of participation in regionally-based technology clubs.*

Improving the skill base

6.12 Good management means competent, trained managers. There have been substantial changes in management training in recent years. The Management Charter Initiative (MCI), an employer-led organisation supported by Employment Department (ED), has developed standards for managers at different levels based on wide, practical experience. These are reflected in NVQs.

6.13 These qualifications point individual managers and employers to what is needed in an effective manager. They provide a target to work towards and a framework within which skills can be assessed and recognised by individuals or existing and prospective employers. Some 40,000 managers are working towards management NVQs and many others are using the management standards, which underlie the NVQs, as part of their training and development. Improvements in performance and profitability can be seen in businesses using management NVQs.

6.14 ED has developed Investors in People to give recognition to employers who meet the highest standards in the development of people, including managers. Companies who are Investors in People integrate staff development with business objectives. They benefit from the development of all their employees.

Engineers and Engineering

6.15 Engineering underpins many sectors of industry. Adopting best practice and improving management skills in engineering is important. Engineers play a crucial role in developing and adapting new technology. Engineering can offer a rewarding career to our best young people. But they will only be encouraged into engineering if UK firms better utilise and reward engineering skills at all levels.

6.16 Improving UK competitiveness through better use of engineering requires:

- the Government, the engineering profession and industry to promote all levels of engineering careers in schools;

- industry to make better use of engineers, giving them, for instance, broader and earlier responsibility;

- industry to train more technicians, supervisors and craft workers whilst improving the quality of training to best international standards;

- universities, employers and the engineering profession to broaden engineering formation by including elements of management, finance, languages and personal skills throughout education and career development; and

- the Government and the engineering profession to enhance the understanding and status of engineering at Board level in companies, among financial institutions, and opinion formers.

6.17 Responsibility for change rests primarily with companies and the professional bodies which represent engineers. Much is already happening, but these activities lack coherence and coordination. The Government is helping. For example:

- from September 1994, the Government is introducing engineering bursaries to encourage students with good A levels to choose engineering degree courses; and

- working closely with engineering organisations, the Welsh Office has helped create the new Engineering Centre for Wales.

Improving access to help

6.18 Managers in smaller companies are skilled in some areas but their lack of experience in others may threaten the success of their business. They are by nature independent and may be reluctant to seek outside help and doubtful about its quality and relevance. If they do decide they want help they frequently do not know where to go. Many services are available but they are of variable quality and there is no common access point. Those access points that do exist are often inconvenient for the customer. Moreover most existing services are designed for start-ups. Relatively few are available for the established company.

6.19 The Government therefore invited TECs in England to bring together partnerships of all local business support agencies to establish a network of one-stop shops, called Business Links, for information and business development services. DTI is providing pump priming finance for the establishment of the Business Link network. It is also contributing to the cost of many services and expects to continue to do so via its funding of TEC enterprise activities and the provision of DTI services through Business Links.

BUSINESS LINKS

By early May 21 Business Links were open and over 50 are expected by the end of 1994. The aim, by the end of 1995, is a network which covers all parts of England, building up to about 200 outlets, all accredited as meeting high quality service standards and maintaining them.

Services include:

- *Personal Business Advisers to work with a company over a period to help identify its needs and assemble a support package*
- *information and advice on:*
  - *business strategy and change*
  - *financial management, late payment, taxation and availability of grants*
  - *regulatory requirements*
  - *the Single Market*
  - *training and development*
  - *business start-up*
  - *other business information, and databases*
- *export services*
- *consultancy*
- *innovation, quality, design and technology services*
- *awareness events*
- *training courses*
- *business "health checks"*

6.20 When the network of Business Links is complete, every company will have a local point of access to a wide range of services which Personal Business Advisers will put together and tailor to its needs. Business Links will seek out companies which they can help. Their focus will be smaller companies with potential to grow, usually with 10-200 employees. They will take responsibility for giving advice on customers' problems, not just refer them on to someone else if they do not have an immediate answer.

6.21 In Scotland most of these services are already provided through the Enterprise bodies and their network of lecs.

New Initiatives

Best practice

6.22 The CBI and DTI are conducting a study of 100 of the best UK companies to identify links between external influences on companies and best practice in management and innovation. The results of the study will be announced by the end of September 1994.

6.23 The Engineering Employers' Federation has developed a programme with member companies, the University of Warwick Manufacturing Group and the CBI which focuses on how companies can best develop their people to become more competitive.

6.24 The Government will establish a regional network which will promote best practice in supply chain partnerships to include buyers and suppliers in both the private and public sectors.

REGIONAL SUPPLY NETWORK

In England the proposed regional supply network will:
- *provide information on sourcing opportunities for buyers and sellers*
- *help companies exploit new opportunities in both public and private sectors*
- *help small firms to expand their customer base*
- *work with Business Links to improve the quality of local suppliers*

In Wales:
- *Source Wales seeks world-wide sourcing opportunities and helps suppliers to meet demands of world-class customers*

In Scotland:
- *the Enterprise networks are helping supplier companies achieve the most demanding customer requirements*

6.25 BS5750 certification was introduced in the late 1970s. Together with product certification standards it has made a significant contribution to raising quality. It is important that industry makes best use of both approaches in its drive for total quality. DTI and BSI are working with industry to develop these standards further to promote continuous improvement.

6.26 The Government will encourage sectoral best practice in new ways. For example, encouraged by DTI, engineering companies, through their Trade Associations and lenders (finance companies and banks) are exploring ways of benchmarking the quality of capital investment in smaller companies.

> **TOURISM**
>
> *Tourism is one of the UK's leading industries. The international market place is growing and becoming more competitive. But the UK's market share is falling.*
>
> *The National Tourist Boards have been addressing the strengths and weaknesses of the industry. Recognising its importance, the CBI is setting up a "Tourism Action Group" to work in partnership with the National Tourist Boards and the industry to seek improvements in competitiveness. Priorities will include:*
> - *creation of world class standards of quality and value*
> - *improvement in career appeal and training to raise service standards*
> - *the needs of tourists in the transport infrastructure*
> - *the regulatory and tax environment*

Improving the skill base

6.27 The Government intends to build on the early success of management NVQs by offering funding to ensure the NVQs are kept up to date and widely used by employers.

> **IMPROVING MANAGEMENT SKILLS**
> - *MCI will review the management content of NVQs, drawing on experience so far. In particular a flexible "core and options" approach will be explored*
> - *TECs will be encouraged to promote improvements in management training among smaller companies*
> - *The case for targets for management development will be considered*
> - *MCI will identify and publicise examples of good practice in management training in smaller firms*
> - *The Government will look to the Business Schools and others to contribute to improving the skill base by continued improvement in the relevance and quality of courses*

6.28 The actions described above will be taken into account in the Welsh strategy on skills and enterprise to be issued later this year, and in the current review of Scottish training policy. In Northern Ireland, the Training and Employment Agency will continue to place a high priority on management development and training.

6.29 As part of an effort towards unification, the engineering bodies are proposing to move to a new structure which will provide a single voice at national level and enhance cooperation at a regional and local level. The main proposals are:

- the establishment of a reformed Engineering Council, with democratically elected members, which within a single structure will work through two boards to deal with the regulation and the promotion of the profession; and

- the establishment of Regional Engineering Centres in major cities to pool the resources of the various institutions.

6.30 The Government welcomes these proposals and the profession's commitment to further development within this framework. It expects to see rapid progress.

Improving access to help

6.31 To provide continuity in funding and services DTI will offer rolling three year funding to TECs which have established strong partnerships in their area, are making satisfactory progress in setting up Business Links and have obtained a three year licence from their Government Regional Office. The new Personal Business Adviser service is central to Business Links. DTI will be reviewing experience in early Business Links so as to maximise the effectiveness of the service and will extend its funding to help meet the on-going costs of the service after the pump-priming period.

6.32 Currently most DTI services are available through Government Regional Offices. In future, as the network develops, Business Links will become the normal point of entry for DTI services, which will all carry the Business Link name when delivered through Business Links. In England, other Government departments will increasingly make their services available through Business Links.

BUSINESS LINKS: FURTHER DEVELOPMENTS
- *Diagnostic and consultancy service to help smaller companies analyse and improve their businesses, including any necessary consultancy*
- *Consultancy brokerage service to advise on choice and use of quality assured consultants*
- *Help and advice for suppliers*
- *Growing range of export services, especially for new exporters*
- *Innovation and technology counsellors in all Business Links beginning with an initial pilot of 20**
- *Innovation credits**
- *Access to local and national networks of expertise on innovation and technology, and overseas technology and best practice**
- *Design advice*
- *Promotion of Investors in People and help for smaller companies to obtain the standard*

*See chapter on Innovation

6.33 The Scottish Business Shops will provide a local first point of access to these and other services. In Wales, a Prospectus will soon be published inviting proposals for the improvement of the delivery of business services.

6.34 The Government's commitment to Business Links is clear. The aim now is to complete by the end of 1995 a network of high quality Business Links covering the whole of England and to increase the effectiveness of business support arrangements to improve the competitiveness of our companies.

INNOVATION

7.1 Innovation – the successful exploitation of new ideas – is essential for sustained competitiveness and wealth creation. A country aiming to keep ahead of its competitors needs companies which innovate. Successful innovation requires good management, appropriate finance, skills and a supportive overall climate.

INNOVATING COMPANIES OUTPERFORM THEIR COMPETITORS[1]

- *Innovating firms grow faster than non-innovators, especially in periods of recession*
- *Innovators are more profitable than non-innovators*
- *Companies with single innovations are unable to sustain above average performance – those with a process of continuing innovation can sustain above average sales, growth and profitability*

How does the UK measure up?

7.2 Many companies and some sectors are world class:

- UK consumption of medicines accounts for just over 3 per cent of the world market, yet the UK produces 5 per cent of the world's needs and is responsible for 8 per cent of R&D expenditure. The research for six out of the top 20 best selling drugs in 1991 and 1992 was carried out in the UK;

- at the end of 1993, 166 biotechnology companies, with a combined turnover of more than £400 million, spent £130 million on R&D. These are forecast[2] to rise to over £870 million and £200 million respectively by 1996;

- the UK aeronautics industry is a leader in design and manufacture of advanced systems – the first advanced "fly-by-light" control systems in use anywhere in the world were developed in the UK; and

- a medium sized UK company has won 40 per cent of the world market with an innovative gas sensing product. It invests 5 per cent of its turnover in R&D.

But other sectors need to improve significantly, and even market leaders must continue to improve their performance.

[1] Geroski and Machin; *Do Innovating Firms Outperform Non-Innovators? (An analysis of 500 quoted UK firms)*. [Business Strategy Review] (Summer 1992)

[2] *UK biotech '94 – the way area: A strategic review in conjunction with the UK Bioindustry Association*. [Arthur Anderson] (1994)

7.3 The need for improvement is shown in a number of ways:

- UK industrial R&D expenditure as a proportion of GDP has fallen behind that of some other leading economies (chart 7.1). Total UK expenditure on R&D has also declined relative to that of our main competitors;

- the UK has a declining share of US patents (chart 7.2). Our relative advantage is slipping in some traditional sectors. Others, such as fine chemicals, have shown a significant improvement over the last two decades;

- technical qualifications tend to be less common and less well rewarded in UK industry than in that of other countries[3]; and

- one third of a sample of companies surveyed in 1992 had not introduced new technology (automation or flexible manufacturing systems) since 1989 and had no plans to do so[4].

7.4 Innovation is about the successful exploitation of all new ideas, whether they are major cultural, organisational or technological changes, or incremental improvements to keep one step ahead. Scientific and technological advances can be an important element of innovation, but developments across the whole range of industrial and commercial activities, for example design and marketing are also important. These are challenges for all companies, not just those in manufacturing.

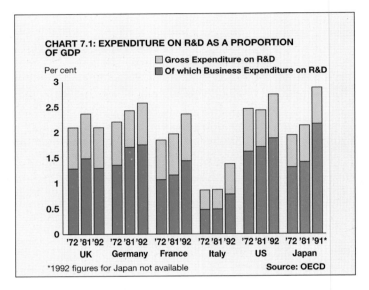

CHART 7.1: EXPENDITURE ON R&D AS A PROPORTION OF GDP

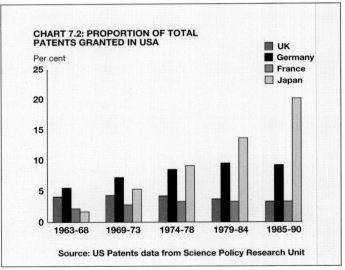

CHART 7.2: PROPORTION OF TOTAL PATENTS GRANTED IN USA

---

[3] O'Mahony; *Productivity Levels in British and German Manufacturing Industry.* [National Institute Economic Review No.139] (1992)

[4] *Made in the UK – The Survey of British Manufacturers.* [Coopers and Lybrand] (1992)

7.5 Successful companies need not only new ideas, but also good management to turn those ideas into commercially attractive products which their customers want to buy.

The challenge to companies

7.6 To become more innovative, companies need to:

- change the climate within their organisation to stimulate innovation;

- develop their people, equipment and processes by training, investing in new technology, and comparing themselves with leading companies (benchmarking);

- take advantage of external skills and know-how; and

- increase their use, adaptation and development of novel processes and products, including greater collaboration with universities and other research organisations.

7.7 Many private sector organisations, such as Research and Technology Organisations (RTOs), provide active support for innovation by companies. Companies themselves have also set up networks which share business knowledge, skills and technology. "Innovation NorthWest" is an example of a large and expanding network of companies and private organisations running self-sustaining activities.

The Government's contribution

7.8 The Government assists companies to improve their innovative performance in a number of ways. As described in chapter 4, it helps, through the education and training system, to provide the workforce with the necessary skills. It contributes to the provision of an efficient scientific and technological infrastructure by setting common standards for measurement, materials and quality (chapter 13). In addition:

- it provides funding for R&D undertaken by the science and engineering base (universities and research establishments); for R&D commissioned by Government departments; and for R&D undertaken through European programmes; and

- it contributes to setting a favourable climate for innovation, and helps companies obtain advice and support for innovation.

Follow up to the Science, Engineering and Technology White Paper

7.9 Last year's White Paper – Realising Our Potential[5] – set out Government policy on the contribution of UK science, engineering and technology to competitiveness. The White Paper:

- emphasised the importance of partnership between business, the science and engineering communities and Government; and

- explained how Government resources would be directed to the best interests of the UK economy.

7.10 The Technology Foresight Programme – a key initiative in the White Paper – will help to identify opportunities by examining both market developments and technological capabilities within the UK over the next two decades. This will enable both Government and industry to make better informed decisions and will improve awareness and networking.

TECHNOLOGY FORESIGHT PROGRAMME: PROGRESS

- *Establishment of Steering Group consisting of leading industrialists and academics, chaired by the Chief Scientific Adviser*
- *Establishment of market-led foresight panels in 15 sectors:*
  Agriculture, Natural Resources and Environment
  Manufacturing, Production and Business Processes
  Defence and Aerospace
  Materials
  Chemicals
  Construction
  Financial Services
  Food and Drink
  Health and Life Sciences
  Energy
  Transport
  Communications
  Leisure and Education
  IT and Electronics
  Retail and Distribution
- *The panels will report early in 1995. They will consult widely, in many cases with a strong regional element*

---

[5] *Realising Our Potential: A strategy for Science, Engineering and Technology.* Cm2250 [HMSO] (1993)

7.11 The White Paper committed departments with significant Science and Technology (S&T) expenditure to take account of wealth creation in pursuit of their objectives. This expenditure amounted to £2.9 billion in 1992/3. The annual Government Forward Look[6] (recently published for the first time) sets out departments' long term S&T strategies and outlines examples of how this is already being achieved. In future, strategies will be informed by Technology Foresight and will draw on the views of the Council for Science and Technology, which brings together top academics and industrialists to advise the Government.

7.12 In addition, as announced in the White Paper, the Research Councils have been restructured in a manner consistent with the new partnership between industry and Government. They are now required to consider how they can contribute to wealth creation through meeting the needs of all potential users of their research. The Councils now have Chairmen drawn from industry, and a membership which includes strong industrial representation.

7.13 Universities and academics need more effective incentives for industrially relevant work. The White Paper made clear that the Research Councils and Higher Education Funding Councils (HEFCs) will be expected, when setting priorities and allocating resources, to give appropriate recognition to the relevance as well as the excellence of proposed research.

7.14 The White Paper explained how firms and research bodies can gain access to a range of funding sources, both national and European. The Government has worked actively to ensure that the fourth EC R&D Framework Programme serves UK interests well. It will be contributing on average £360 million a year from 1995 to 1998, compared with £250 million a year for the third Framework Programme.

7.15 The importance of partnership between industry and Government emphasised in the White Paper is illustrated by the National Strategic Technology Acquisition Plan, prepared by the aeronautics industry. Meeting the industry's future technological requirements requires the effective use of all the available public and private funds.

Government Help for Companies

7.16 Innovation is ultimately the responsibility of companies. Only they can bring together the resources, investment and skills for market success. Companies carry out most of the UK's R&D, which not only leads to new products and processes but also develops the firm's capacity to use new ideas from elsewhere. Our inventiveness is

---

[6] *The Forward Look of Government-funded Science, Engineering and Technology.* [HMSO] (1994)

widely acknowledged but the commercial exploitation of ideas has been disappointing. Innovation is not just about R&D or new technology. It concerns the successful exploitation of any new ideas, involving all aspects of business.

7.17 There are, however, several ways in which the Government can encourage companies to use available resources to innovate more effectively.

The Climate for Innovation

7.18 A favourable climate for innovation rests on a close dialogue between Government, industry and providers of finance. The Finance for Business chapter explains how the Government is encouraging the provision of finance for growing companies. Through its industrial secondees, DTI's strengthened Innovation Unit aims to change attitudes within the public and private sectors in favour of innovation. Other Government departments are closely involved with similar work.

EXAMPLES OF INNOVATION UNIT ACTIVITIES

* *Annual scoreboard of company R&D expenditure*
* *Successful development of regional business networks*
* *Stronger local university-industry linkages*
* *Identification of innovation best practice*
* *Substantial coverage of innovation by quality national and local media*
* *"Wealth from Science & Engineering" teaching materials in over 4000 secondary schools*
* *Annual Innovation Lecture attended by over 1000 top people*

7.19 Other measures aim to raise the general awareness of innovation more widely. The Office of Science and Technology is promoting public understanding of science, engineering and technology, and the relaunched Design Council plays an important role in promoting awareness of design issues.

7.20 The regulatory framework influences the general climate for innovation. The Department of the Environment (DoE) and Industry departments are working to stimulate an effective business response to environmental regulation and emergent opportunities through the Environmental Best Practice Scheme.

The Process of Innovation

7.21 Companies must manage innovation effectively. Many Government funded activities offer support. These include the spread of best innovation practice and awareness of technological opportunities, provision of advice and help, and benchmarking of business processes.

7.22 The exchange of people is often the best way to encourage the spread of best practice, skills and technology. The Government and the Research Councils promote a greater two-way flow of people between industry and universities. This helps companies take up and benefit from new developments.

PARTNERSHIPS BETWEEN INDUSTRY AND UNIVERSITIES

- *Funding of universities by business has grown from about £30 million to £120 million over the past decade*

Government helps to support:

- *250,000 students and 20,000 companies involved in enterprise related training at any one time*
- *3,000 research students working on joint projects with firms*
- *over 70 universities and 700 firms now engaged in collaborative research*
- *500 current technology transfer partnerships, between University departments and companies, employing new graduates in industry. Some 30 per cent of these companies employ fewer than 50 people*

Advice and Services

7.23 Companies increasingly use external sources of technology. Many organisations are available in the UK to provide information and expertise.

7.24 Some innovation support services are available to firms locally. These include colleges of further education, TECs, patent agents or database providers, as well as other companies in the region which can offer help and advice.

7.25 Companies can also get help from a range of national organisations providing innovation support, including university centres of excellence, financial institutions, RTOs, the Patent Office or EC Relay Centres.

7.26 It is also important that companies have access to international research programmes and to new insights, practices and technology developed overseas. Government helps companies keep in touch with developments and opportunities abroad through its overseas technical services.

7.27 Business Links are increasingly acting as a unifying access point in England for all the available support, particularly for smaller firms. Equivalent arrangements are being developed in Scotland through the network of Business Shops; through the Industrial Research and Technology Unit in Northern Ireland; and similar business centres are under consideration in Wales.

The Acquisition, Development and Use of Technology

7.28 Government funding for science, engineering and technology is increasingly contributing to competitiveness through the measures announced in last year's White

Paper. Industry's substantial R&D effort builds on this. In addition, the Government promotes the uptake and development of technology through:

- support for a range of activities promoting technology use and adaptation through collaborative R&D, adaptation projects or technology demonstration;

- schemes offering financial support for innovation in smaller businesses;

- work with RTOs, through a framework agreed with the Association of Independent RTOs, to aid support for innovation, particularly for smaller companies; and

- improved access to EC programmes, again particularly for smaller firms. This involves Government departments and EC Relay Centres and will be more vigorously promoted through Business Links.

New Initiatives

7.29 The Government will further help innovation in the UK through a number of initiatives. It will improve the **climate for innovation:**

- by working with the City and financial institutions, DTI will bring together six sectoral working groups to produce practical guidelines and develop a common understanding of the nature of risks and rewards involved in innovation amongst company managers, analysts and investors; and

- DoE and DTI, in consultation with interested parties, will stimulate the free exchange of information between Government, industry, and regulators, including the large amount of information on best available technologies held by Her Majesty's Inspectorate of Pollution.

7.30 The Government will help the **process of innovation** by stimulating the exchange of people between industry and Universities and colleges:

- the successful Teaching Company Scheme (TCS) will be extended, in close consultation with industry, and new Teaching Company Centres developed to help smaller firms benefit from the skills of graduates; and

- the Government will consider options for a scheme, similar to TCS, to promote the transfer of people at technician level from Further Education Institutions to local companies.

7.31 The Government will improve **access to advice and services** by providing more services through Business Links, by supporting networks of support organisations at local and national level, and by providing access to global developments:

- Innovation and Technology Counsellors will be funded in the first 20 Business Links to provide advice and guidance to companies on innovation. Based on the experience of these pilots, the Government intends to fund Counsellors in the complete Business Link network;

- "Innovation Credits" will be introduced and made available through Business Links. They will encourage smaller firms to discover the value of outside help by offsetting the cost for first-time users. The credits will be worth up to £1000 per year per company;

- networks of local contacts ("Nearnet") will be established across the UK to enable local sources of innovation support to be brought together in a coherent way. Business Links will increasingly facilitate access to such networks, paying particular attention to helping smaller firms participate;

- similarly, national centres of expertise will be linked through an actively-managed network ("Supernet") being developed by DTI. The network will include a database of expertise and information for companies, again accessible through Business Links; and

- DTI's overseas technology services will be expanded to cover a wider range of sectors, professional disciplines and countries. They will be made more accessible through Business Links in England, and other suitable bodies in Scotland and Wales. Pilot schemes will be established to enable firms to have prompt and more direct access to the latest ideas and developments overseas.

7.32 The Government will also improve the **development and use of technology** by helping to improve the chances of commercial success of new products:

- smaller companies receiving Government support for innovation will also receive help to find sources of private finance and sources of assistance in developing business skills.

7.33 The Government will strengthen **industry and University partnerships** by further building on the initiatives announced in last year's White Paper:

- Higher Education Institutions will increasingly receive financial recognition from the HEFCs for research conducted in partnership with industry. This will amount to a significant proportion of the relevant income from industry. The proportion of the HEFCs' agreed total budgets used for this purpose will increase;

- individual academics will be rewarded for undertaking collaborative work with industry through the recently introduced Realising our Potential Awards;

- the HEFCs will take full account of the results of the Technology Foresight Programme in allocating funds between subjects; and

- the next Research Assessment Exercise by the HEFCs will include full recognition of high quality research undertaken in partnership with industry.

FAIR AND OPEN MARKETS

8.1 This chapter looks at how the Government – through trade policy, export promotion, measures to combat unfair subsidies and state aids, and inward and outward investment – can help British business compete more effectively in international markets.

TRADE POLICY

Removing barriers and opening doors

8.2 UK business cannot keep pace with international competitors without easy access to overseas markets. It also needs advanced and competitively priced inputs to its production processes. As business becomes more complex and globalised, the remaining barriers to trade and investment are the more disruptive and damaging. Eliminating barriers benefits UK business and consumers in terms of choice and price for goods and services competitively supplied in open markets.

UK trade policy – the international context

8.3 UK trade policy operates as part of the EC's Common Commercial Policy. The EC operates within the multilateral system of the GATT, now being taken further in the new World Trade Organisation (WTO). Over a hundred countries are GATT members and many others are negotiating to join. The GATT system enables countries to negotiate mutual reductions of trade barriers such as customs duties. It prohibits trade discrimination and provides remedies against unfair trading practices. EC trade policy is also governed by a network of bilateral treaties, notably with countries in the wider Europe and the Mediterranean Basin.

8.4 In influencing EC trade policy the UK works closely with other Member States. All Member States are becoming more dependent on world as well as European markets for goods and services as shown by the broad support within the EC for the Uruguay Round of GATT talks.

8.5 However, protectionism is far from ended. Average tariff levels in industrialised countries have fallen from about 40 per cent in the late 1940s to about 5 per cent now. They will fall further as a result of the GATT Round. Nevertheless, non-tariff barriers appear to have increased between the mid-1960s and the mid-1980s. That period saw, in particular, the development of Common Agricultural Policy (CAP) restrictions, of textile quotas under the Multifibre Arrangement and of US and EC restraints on imports of cars. Estimates by World Bank economists suggest that over this period the proportion of developed country imports affected by non-tariff barriers rose from around a quarter to nearly a half. This proportion should, however, decline as the results of the GATT Round are progressively implemented.

8.6 Non-tariff barriers currently confronting UK exporters include not only overt restrictions on imports but also such measures as discriminatory excise duties, subsidies and government procurement; and troublesome regulatory measures governing restrictive practices, technical standards and the like. Discriminatory liquor taxes in Japan and Chile, subsidies to national airlines in France and Spain, preferential Government procurement in the United States, and protection of financial and other services in a number of countries in East and South East Asia are just some examples of the difficulties our exporters face.

8.7 Agricultural trade is also distorted by the support policies operated in developed countries. Such policies have insulated agriculture from market forces and held back competitiveness both internationally, by preventing comparative advantage from operating, and domestically, by distorting resource use. The EC is no exception, with the level of support under the CAP being close to the OECD average.

The Government's approach

8.8 The Government aims to improve access to world markets through further reductions in trade barriers. It welcomes the strong support for open trade from the private sector and will maintain the close partnership with business enjoyed throughout the Uruguay Round negotiations.

8.9 UK trade policy strategy must be focused on using our influence in the EC. The UK must work through the Council of Ministers to persuade other Member States and the Commission and supplement these efforts through informal bilateral diplomacy both within and outside the EC.

8.10 The agenda may be summarised as follows:

- **within the EC** the Government seeks to ensure that the Single Market rules are implemented and enforced. DTI's Single Market Compliance Unit pursues specific complaints from UK business and more general enforcement problems. DTI is also launching a new guide[1] for UK firms on how to get Single Market problems sorted out;

- **in the wider Europe** the Government works for genuine free trade under EC Association agreements and for structural reforms in Eastern European countries;

---

[1] *The Single Market: Making it work for you.* [DTI] (forthcoming)

- **in the rest of the world** the Government presses for adherence to GATT disciplines on protection and discrimination and for further negotiated dismantling of barriers.

8.11 The UK worked hard to get a worthwhile agricultural package in the Uruguay Round. Together with CAP reform, this will result in lower protection in the medium term. In the longer term agriculture is now within the GATT and the new WTO framework. The Government will press for further reductions in support for agriculture in the EC and more widely.

The future

8.12 The Uruguay Round has achieved significant tariff reductions, tightened existing disciplines on unilateral protection, and streamlined arbitration and retaliation provisions. GATT will cover agriculture, services and intellectual property effectively for the first time. The new WTO will oversee the results. The Government's first priority is to secure implementation of these improvements in market access. It will also work to ensure that the new WTO rapidly becomes fully effective. More specifically, it will press for:

- **dismantling of remaining legitimate barriers.** In some cases further negotiations will continue the Uruguay Round process: the UK will pursue this vigorously in areas such as financial services, telecommunications, maritime services, aerospace and steel. The Government will continue to argue for liberalisation and deregulation;

- **delivery of real market opening by new countries joining GATT/WTO.** Before applicant countries like China and Taiwan get full rights under GATT/WTO, they will have to give commitments on the introduction of market mechanisms, deregulation and genuine non-discrimination, as well as on tariffs and services;

- **vigorous EC use of new GATT/WTO** provisions for arbitration and (multilaterally authorised) retaliation against barriers which breach GATT/WTO obligations. This is the key to resolving outstanding trade problems like liquor tax discrimination in Asia and Latin America;

- **work in the WTO on new trade issues,** particularly trade and the environment, to promote open markets and to discourage trade restrictions; and

- **disciplined recourse to commercial defence** by the EC. This covers temporary sectoral safeguard restrictions where there are surges of imports;

countervailing and anti-dumping duties on unfair trade which is subsidised or sold below home market price; and other multilaterally authorised retaliation. The Government will support cases when there is justification on economic grounds for doing so, taking full account of UK producer, consumer and industrial user interests.

STATE AIDS

8.13 Howard Davies, the CBI's Director-General, has said:

"It is a serious misuse of resources for Member States to divert taxpayers' money to subsidise uneconomic production by loss-making enterprises. State subsidies distort competition, weaken efficient producers and ultimately put firms and jobs at risk".[2]

8.14 The Government entirely agrees. It owes it to UK industry to ensure that its increasing competitiveness in world markets is not undermined by unfair subsidies given by other governments. Nor should our attraction as a location for international investment be undermined.

The Government's strategy

8.15 Worldwide information on subsidies provided by governments is not available. However, it is clear that many of our major competitors, including within the EC, provide substantial aid, direct and indirect, to their industries.

8.16 The Government cannot and should not simply match what others offer. To do so would be an uneconomic use of scarce resources, and would have unacceptable consequences for public expenditure. The UK needs to work multilaterally to secure common binding rules, both internationally and in the EC. The Government's strategy is to work to reduce the volume of aid given and for greater transparency through a progressive tightening of the EC state aids rules. Much has already been done. Last December the European Council committed itself to the vigorous application of EC state aids rules.

The next steps

The GATT

8.17 In the Uruguay Round the UK worked hard and successfully to strengthen subsidies arrangements. From 1995, the new GATT Subsidies Agreement will provide

[2] CBI statement on launch of CBI report – see footnote on page 86

for quicker and more effective disciplines against abuse. For the first time developing countries will be required to accept obligations on subsidies. The Government will press for full implementation of this agreement, and for the resolution of outstanding issues on steel and civil aircraft subsidies.

The European Community

8.18 Articles 92 and 93 of the Treaty of Rome provide the basis for the control of state aids within the EC. The Commission has built on these to set out the aid rules for particular sectors. This increasingly vigorous approach has been well supported by the decisions of the European Court of Justice. The UK fully supports the Commission in efforts to reduce distorting aid.

8.19 Priorities for further action are:

- to ensure effective constraints on "subsidy auctions" for internationally mobile investment projects, particularly those that simply transfer jobs from one part of the EC to another. The Government is pressing the Commission to adopt its proposal to limit aid for capital intensive projects;

- clearer Commission guidelines on the acceptable boundaries of "grey" areas of state aids which may increasingly damage competition as more direct aids are curbed. Examples are special tax arrangements, training and employment aids and preferential arrangements for the leasing or provision of land and buildings;

- tighter and more effective control of aid to specific industry sectors, such as steel and shipbuilding;

- the extension of Commission monitoring of aid for publicly owned manufacturing companies to cover publicly owned utilities;

- strict control of subsidies to prevent liberalisation of air transport and shipping being undermined;

- uniform application of state aid rules throughout the new European Economic Area;

- progressive adoption of state aid disciplines by Central and Eastern European countries;

- more prompt and determined action by the Commission on agricultural state aids, in particular those that have not been notified;

- greater transparency and swifter handling of complaints by the Commission. More use of the Article 93 (2) procedure would allow those likely to be damaged by state aid to offer views formally to the Commission; and

- more effective action to secure repayment of aid judged to be illegal, including use of Article 171 of the Maastricht Treaty. This allows the Commission to propose fines against Member States proved not to have taken measures necessary to comply with a judgement of the European Court of Justice.

Partnership with industry

8.20 The Government works closely with trade associations and individual companies to identify and pursue complaints about distorting aid offered by other countries. Where necessary, it will press for tighter, or new, rules to protect particular sectors from unfair competition. The initiative taken with the European Commission by the CBI in their recent paper "Controlling State Aids – Making the Single Market Work"[3] is welcomed by the Government.

The Common Agricultural Policy

8.21 Support under the CAP is different from state aids in that it is provided through a Community policy decided by the Council of Ministers. High support prices (although reduced following the 1992 reforms) are provided at the expense of consumers and taxpayers. They and other measures, particularly supply controls, insulate EC agriculture from market forces and reduce its competitiveness by encouraging uneconomic farmers to stay in business.

8.22 The size of farms in the UK is much larger than elsewhere in the Community and the proportion of the workforce in agriculture much lower. Removal of CAP distortions would allow UK agriculture to exploit its competitive advantage within the EC arising from our farm structure, and to expand where it has a comparative advantage.

8.23 The 1992 reforms of the CAP resulted in substantial reductions in support prices. These reductions represented a significant achievement for the UK. However, further substantial price reductions are needed to increase the sensitivity of EC agriculture to market forces. The UK's aim is therefore to continue the reduction in support prices to bring supply and demand into balance. Supply controls can then be removed and market forces operate to improve the competitiveness of the agricultural and food processing industries. This would remove constraints, such as milk quotas, which tend to divert processing facilities and jobs away from the UK.

[3] *Controlling State Aids – Making the Single Market Work.* [CBI] (1994)

EXPORT PROMOTION

8.24 World trade is set to grow by 5-10 per cent a year over the next decade, helped by the successful completion of the GATT Round. This presents both opportunities and challenges.

8.25 The UK is a successful exporting nation, the world's fifth largest exporter in both goods and services. Since 1981 the volume of UK manufactured exports has grown faster than in France, Germany, Italy and Japan. After decades of decline our share of world trade in goods has stabilised. However, despite success in areas such as financial services, our share in services as a whole is still falling.

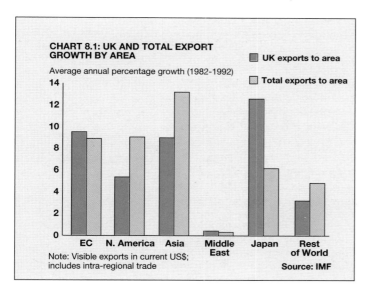

CHART 8.1: UK AND TOTAL EXPORT GROWTH BY AREA

Average annual percentage growth (1982-1992)

■ UK exports to area
□ Total exports to area

EC   N. America   Asia   Middle East   Japan   Rest of World

Note: Visible exports in current US$; includes intra-regional trade

Source: IMF

8.26 To meet future challenges, and seize opportunities, we must improve export performance throughout the economy. This applies, for example, in the world's most dynamic and growing markets in Asia (chart 8.1). Success will require a strategic approach to exporting and a willingness to 'benchmark' against the world's best.

Government Support for Exporters

8.27 The Government has a key role in providing information, advice and support for exporters, drawing on the resources of diplomatic posts overseas and an expanding support network at home. An independent US assessment of export assistance services in a number of European countries concluded that the UK had "developed perhaps the most clearly presented and coherently marketed package of export assistance programmes"[4].

8.28 However, improvements will continue to be made. A new Director General of Export Promotion has been appointed to lead the Overseas Trade Services (OTS), a joint operation of the DTI and the FCO and the main deliverer of export promotion services. The OTS has been strengthened. Each of our top 80 export markets has a dedicated export promotion unit complementing the commercial work undertaken in 200 FCO Posts overseas. The FCO allocates more resources to commercial work than to any other activity. Over 75 private sector Export Promoters have been seconded to OTS. Using their skills and experience, OTS is developing Market Plans which will direct the promotional effort for each of the UK's 80 major export markets.

[4] William E. Northdurft; *Going Global.* [Brookings Institute, Washington] (1992)

8.29 All Government departments are giving higher priority to developing strategies to improve their export effort. These strategies, and the wide range of export support already offered, are coordinated by the Whitehall Export Promotion Committee.

GOVERNMENT SUPPORT FOR EXPORTS

Many departments support the export drive:

- *the Overseas Trade Services (OTS), a joint operation by the DTI and FCO supported by the Scottish, Welsh and Northern Ireland departments, provides advice to help UK business secure contracts overseas. With the support of OTS, a consortium led by a major UK company has secured a £500 million bridge contract in Portugal and another UK led consortium has won a £100 million telecom modernisation project in Latvia and taken a major stake in the privatised telecom industry*
- *Ministry of Defence. 1993 was a record year for UK defence exports. Orders exceeded £6 billion, and included the armoured personnel carrier contract in Kuwait, our largest land force deal since the 1970s. More than half our defence export orders last year were on a Government-to-Government basis*
- *DoE has strengthened its support for the export effort of the UK construction industry, which earns about £6 billion overseas. For example, last year, DoE Ministers led the first UK trade mission to the Lebanon for almost 20 years. Six major missions are planned for 1994*
- *HM Treasury helps to sell privatisation experience abroad. Following Treasury-led missions, UK privatised utilities recently won major contracts to supply water to Mexico City and to distribute gas in Chile*
- *the Ministry of Agriculture (MAFF) promotes the UK agri-industry overseas. In recent years, Ministerial missions have helped the industry win orders worth at least £55 million. Working with Food from Britain, MAFF is encouraging UK companies to exploit opportunities in continental supermarket chains*
- *DFE and The British Council work to promote UK education and culture overseas. Overseas students contribute over £1 billion annually to the UK economy. The British Council is a catalyst for overseas earnings of about £500 million a year from teaching English overseas*
- *Scottish Trade International (STI), the Government's export body in Scotland, is being strengthened to exploit export opportunities. In 1993, STI-led initiatives were instrumental in achieving export sales of £70 million*

Export Credit Guarantees

8.30 UK companies in the capital goods and projects sectors are well placed to compete for future opportunities in fast developing overseas markets. The Government has therefore substantially improved facilities offered by the Exports Credits Guarantee Department (ECGD). In particular premium rates have on average been reduced by more than 25 per cent since 1991/92, and further capped for selected markets such as India, Mexico and Poland.

8.31 Cover for markets such as China, Hong Kong, Indonesia and South Africa has been increased by 60 per cent over the past two years and will rise steadily to £3.2 billion of commitments in 1996/97. In addition cover has been made available for 11 new markets over the past year. Reinsurance for short term exports has been increased and extended. In 1992/93 new guarantees for project and capital goods exports rose to £3.8 billion, 80 per cent up on the annual average of the previous five years. This has been exceeded again in 1993/94.

Partnership: the Key to Success

8.32 Further success requires an enhanced joint effort between the Government and business. The Prime Minister, and Ministers from a range of departments, are now more frequently accompanied on overseas visits by teams of businessmen. The advice and support of the business people on the British Overseas Trade Board, and its Area Advisory Groups, have also been vital. They have helped launch successful trade campaigns such as North America Now, Priority Japan and the Indo-British Partnership Initiative.

THE INDO-BRITISH PARTNERSHIP

- *The Indo-British Partnership brings together public and private sectors. Launched during the Prime Minister's visit to India in January 1993, it will increase significantly opportunities for trade and investment. Among contracts signed during the visit, one company won a £114 million contract to supply electrical equipment*
- *OTS, in partnership with the private sector, has reached thousands of small firms with publicity on new opportunities for business with India*
- *A major campaign is under way in India, highlighting the potential for increased partnership with UK industry. In November 1993 over 300 UK companies demonstrated their expertise and technology during Indo-British week in Bombay. The week produced over £1.2 billion of contracts*
- *The Indian Prime Minister made a reciprocal visit to Britain in March this year. During this visit, a UK company signed a Memorandum of Understanding worth £700 million*
- *In 1994 there will be a series of sector based events, including plans for a major promotional event in Delhi in November focusing on smaller firms in high technology industries*

8.33 The Export Promoter initiative epitomises this partnership; many companies have generously seconded their people to help the Government's export drive. This initiative has proved successful and will continue.

8.34 In addition, the Overseas Projects Board has set up a number of sector groups, whose membership includes leading business people, to target overseas projects, advise on the tactics for winning them, and where necessary devise ways of focusing Government support on a single UK bidder for a particular project. These groups will help to ensure that UK suppliers and subcontractors gain the maximum possible benefit from contracts won by larger firms.

8.35 As the Government works with business to improve and extend the various services available to exporters, so business should maximise use of those services and develop a strategic outlook to exporting and investment. Trade Associations, Chambers of Commerce and other business support groups should give priority to the development of high-quality export advice and support.

New Initiatives

8.36 The Government will:

- extend and improve its services to business, through Business Links. A package of promotional services, training and support for exporters will be developed to encourage and help many more companies to become exporters. The existing network of 12 private sector export counsellors in English Chambers of Commerce will be expanded. About 70 of the larger Business Links will have an export counsellor. Their help will be available from all Business Links;

- develop sectoral and locally based export promotion initiatives as part of the 'Celebration of Industry' programmes being piloted in the West Midlands, Kent and elsewhere;

- establish, through OTS, closer working relations with the clearing banks. An important aspect will be a pilot system for referring companies from the banks to OTS; and

- follow up the April launch of the Language for Export Initiative by developing a strategy to encourage businesses to take into account foreign languages and cultural issues in their export plans.

INWARD AND OUTWARD INVESTMENT

8.37 The most successful companies in all countries have high productivity, high levels of investment and strong growth. They often invest overseas. Such investment is increasing rapidly. Competitiveness is improved through inward investment by these successful companies. Outward investment allows UK companies to develop their competitive strength in overseas markets.

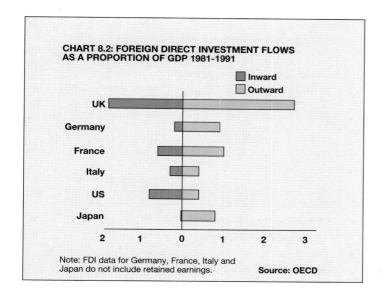

CHART 8.2: FOREIGN DIRECT INVESTMENT FLOWS AS A PROPORTION OF GDP 1981-1991

☐ Inward
☐ Outward

UK
Germany
France
Italy
US
Japan

Note: FDI data for Germany, France, Italy and Japan do not include retained earnings.

Source: OECD

International Comparisons

8.38 During the 1980s, the UK attracted the most investment from overseas and invested most overseas, amongst the G7 countries, as a proportion of GDP (chart 8.2). Japan emerged as an outward investor, although the US remains the most important single investor in the UK. Japan and Germany were major net outward investors. The other countries show a more balanced picture.

INVESTMENT TO AND FROM THE US

The US is easily the biggest foreign investor in the UK, accounting for 42 per cent of the £115 billion invested by foreign companies. There are over 3,500 UK subsidiaries of US companies, among them 96 of the top 100 Fortune companies. They operate in a large number of industrial sectors including industrial machinery, electronics, chemicals and pharmaceuticals, vehicles, food and drink, and banking. US companies have a presence in every area of the UK, although there are concentrations, for example, textiles and clothing in Northern Ireland, banking in London and North West England, electronics in Scotland and South East England, and automotive components in Wales.

The UK is the second biggest foreign investor in the US, accounting for over 20 per cent of the $419 billion invested by foreign companies. The investment is spread across a range of sectors, including chemicals, oil, electrical and mechanical engineering, food and drink, banking, and insurance. Within the manufacturing sector, UK investment stands at over $40 billion, making it the biggest foreign investor.

8.39 UK dominance in inward and outward investment follows from:

- our long history as a trading nation;

- recognition of the benefits of a strong local presence in overseas markets, often involving substantial investment;

- the openness of our economy; and

- integration into the European and global economies.

Inward Investment

8.40 By value of investment, the UK is second only to the US in attracting inward investors (chart 8.3). This success is a major strength in our competitive position.

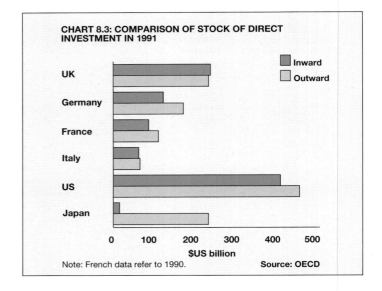

CHART 8.3: COMPARISON OF STOCK OF DIRECT INVESTMENT IN 1991

Note: French data refer to 1990. Source: OECD

8.41 The UK has been more successful than any other European country in attracting inward investment from the US and Japan over the past 40 years (chart 8.4). In recent years the completion of the Single Market has been accompanied by increasing investment from the US and Japan, as their companies sought a base to serve European customers.

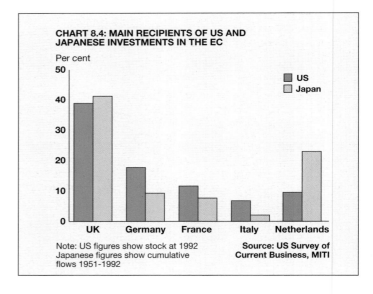

CHART 8.4: MAIN RECIPIENTS OF US AND JAPANESE INVESTMENTS IN THE EC

Note: US figures show stock at 1992 Japanese figures show cumulative flows 1951-1992 Source: US Survey of Current Business, MITI

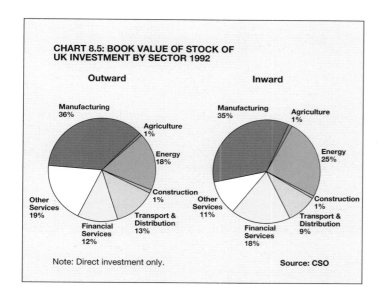

CHART 8.5: BOOK VALUE OF STOCK OF
UK INVESTMENT BY SECTOR 1992

Outward — Inward

Note: Direct investment only.

Source: CSO

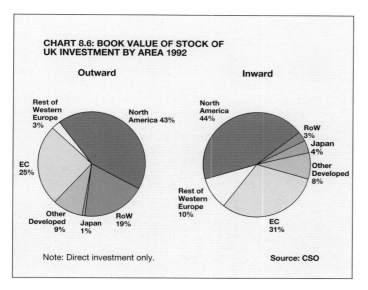

CHART 8.6: BOOK VALUE OF STOCK OF
UK INVESTMENT BY AREA 1992

Outward — Inward

Note: Direct investment only.

Source: CSO

Outward Investment

8.42 By value, we are the world's second largest overseas investor after the US and just in front of Japan. In 1992 this investment was worth £146 billion. Over the last decade, the return on it has been running at about 10 per cent of its value. This investment is mainly in the manufacturing and services field, in the US and EC (charts 8.5 and 8.6). It is clear that most investment has not been aimed at exploiting low labour costs in developing countries.

Competition for Internationally Mobile Investment

8.43 Until the late 1980s, some EC countries did not seek internationally mobile investment. Indeed, some actively discouraged it. Over the last few years, however, competition has intensified. All countries have opened their markets to foreign investment and adopted investor-friendly measures, such as freeing exchange controls, pioneered by the UK. They have also increased their promotional efforts.

8.44 The UK is perceived by inward investors to have many strengths. We score well across a wide range of factors.

SOME OF THE KEY STRENGTHS OF THE UK ACCORDING TO RECENT INVESTORS
- *High labour quality and flexibility*
- *Low overall costs*
- *Low total labour costs*
- *Deregulated business environment*
- *Superior international air services and efficient low cost road transport*
- *Competitive telecommunications*
- *Market proximity*
- *Financial incentives*
- *Low corporate and personal tax rates*
- *The English language and ease of communication*
- *The warmth of welcome and attitude of Government and investment promotion agencies*

The Government's Approach

8.45 Government policy is to encourage both inward and outward investment.

8.46 Inward investment brings world class production techniques, technical innovation and managerial skills, which can be transferred to local companies. It has revived the international competitiveness of some sectors of UK industry, such as vehicles.

IMPACT OF JAPANESE INWARD INVESTMENT IN VEHICLE SECTOR

Japanese inward investment to the UK vehicle industry has been substantial with total planned investment of over £2 billion creating over 7,000 direct jobs. Production capacity has increased by around 400,000 cars (predominantly for export). The indirect benefits have also been profound. The arrival of world-class Japanese manufacturers, with associated component suppliers, in three areas of England (the North East, Derbyshire, the M4 corridor) and North Wales has spurred established producers to greater efforts. Continuous improvement has resulted in higher productivity, improved quality and increased reliability of parts.

The large Japanese UK-based manufacturers buy a substantial proportion of components from European suppliers, and especially from the UK. On reaching full production they will achieve EC content levels of at least 80 per cent. This has already had a major impact on the competitiveness of the UK component sector.

Japanese vehicle manufacturers are also playing a key role in DTI's Learning From Japan initiative, aimed at improving the competitiveness of the UK vehicle component supply industry. This will help second tier component suppliers achieve world standards by learning at first hand from world class Japanese companies.

8.47 Capital expenditure and gross added value per employee are both higher on average for foreign owned than for UK owned companies. Foreign owned companies are among the UK's top exporters. Inward investment can also bring spin-off benefits to suppliers. It can provide new markets and help them to improve quality and expand their product range so that they can compete more effectively in world markets. It raises skill levels in the workforce and brings new jobs.

8.48 Inward investment also contributes to the economic and social development of the area, enhancing it as a location for industry and commerce. These benefits are particularly valuable for Assisted Areas.

8.49 Outward investment can similarly be beneficial for the economy. It generates profits and dividends for the UK. It creates jobs by stimulating exports. It also gains more effective access to world markets for UK goods and services. Research[5] suggests that it has a positive and significant influence on a firm's growth.

8.50 The private sector will invest abroad only if it can take advantage of these potential benefits and so increase turnover and profitability. That decision is for it alone. The Government's policy is to help outward investors by improving the framework within which decisions are made.

How the Government helps

8.51 The UK's promotional system for **inward investment** combines both national and regional agencies in a co-ordinated network. It is a good example of a comprehensive and effective partnership between central and local government and the private sector.

8.52 UK promotion is carried out by the Invest in Britain Bureau (IBB) of DTI. Most of the overseas visiting and promotional activity falls to the Foreign and Commonwealth Office. Scotland, Wales and Northern Ireland have their own agencies. These play an important part in the national effort through targeted promotion, using permanent overseas representatives. These activities are enhanced through the active role of Ministers in meeting potential and existing investors at home and overseas.

8.53 In England there are six Regional Development Organisations (RDOs) covering the regions including most of the English Assisted Areas. They will shortly be joined by one covering Greater London. In addition to government funding, the RDOs have significant local private sector finance and membership, as well as Local Authority support. RDOs are the means of harnessing the contributions of universities, TECs, and other organisations. They help investors get established and encourage them to add more value.

[5] A Silberston: *British Manufacturing Investment Overseas.* [Methuen] (1985)

INWARD INVESTMENT IN SCOTLAND, WALES AND NORTHERN IRELAND.

For many years **Scotland** *has been a major beneficiary of inward investment. This has made a substantial contribution to the transformation of the industrial base.*

- *Of the 18 new plant investments announced by US investors in 1992, eight were in Scotland*
- *Of the 526,000 jobs associated with foreign direct investment in the UK since 1979, 16.5 per cent were created in Scotland*
- *In 1992 employment in overseas owned manufacturing plants in Scotland was around 82,000, representing a quarter of total manufacturing employment*
- *Net capital investment by overseas manufacturing firms in Scotland in 1990 totalled some £423 million, almost a third of total manufacturing investment*
- *In 1990, gross value added per employee in overseas owned manufacturing firms in Scotland was estimated to be two-thirds higher than in UK owned firms located there*
- *Overseas owned firms are particularly dominant in the electronics industry. Scotland produces 26 per cent of Europe's output of personal computers; three out of five of Europe's workstations; 12 per cent of Europe's semiconductors; and over 50 per cent of Europe's automated banking machines. Electronics and electrical engineering is now Scotland's largest export earner*

Inward investment has had a particularly beneficial impact in **Wales**, *where the economy has made a very successful transformation away from dependence on coal and steel.*

- *One third of the manufacturing workforce is now employed by overseas owned companies in modern and efficient factories, many of which have shown their competitiveness by expanding, often more than once*
- *Consumer electronics has been a growth sector. The factories of major household names are located in South Wales along the M4 corridor and in North-East Wales. Initial investment in manufacturing has been followed in some cases by the provision of R&D facilities and other value added activities*
- *Inward investment has helped employment in electronics in Wales to increase by over 40 per cent since 1979*

Northern Ireland *has a long tradition of attracting overseas investment.*

- *In 1992/93 Northern Ireland attracted some 14 per cent of all new investment into the UK, and overseas companies invested a total of £257 million in 27 separate projects which will create over 3200 jobs*
- *Since the first Japanese investment in the mid-1980s, employment in Japanese-owned companies in Northern Ireland has risen to over 2000*
- *As far as the US is concerned, one of the world's top ten chemical firms first set up in Northern Ireland in 1960 and now employs about 1000 people. It continues to invest, including two recent projects to open major R&D operations at a cost of £12 million*

8.54 The Government has taken a wide range of measures to help **outward investment.** It has signed over 60 Investment Promotion and Protection Agreements (IPPAs) since 1975. They create a climate of confidence for investors. They provide for prompt, adequate and effective payment of compensation in the event of expropriation, and for independent settlement of disputes. As international competition for investment has increased, more IPPAs have been successfully negotiated.

8.55 ECGD operates an Overseas Investment Insurance Scheme to provide cover for investors against the risks of expropriation, war or restrictions on remittances to the UK. At the end of 1992/93 ECGD had 86 agreements in force in 35 different countries.

8.56 Double taxation agreements are of major importance for UK overseas investment. They assist taxpayers to trade or invest abroad without the deterrent of double taxation or excessive compliance problems. The UK has the world's largest network of bilateral tax treaties (91 at end-1993) and the number is likely to reach 100 by the end of 1994.

8.57 DTI and FCO Posts overseas provide an advisory and signposting service to potential outward investors. They are currently running a pilot study of an Overseas Investment Enquiry Service in 30 overseas markets, and a Strategic Alliance Service (match-making between medium sized UK and US companies) in the US.

New Initiatives

Inward Investment

8.58 The Government has recently reinforced promotion of inward investment:

- Lord Walker is now personal advisor on inward investment to the President of the Board of Trade;

- a new Chief Executive post has been created to head the IBB; and

- an "aftercare" programme for existing investors is being initiated in England and increased in intensity in Scotland, Wales and Northern Ireland.

8.59 The Government will now take the following measures:

Incentives

- Regional Selective Assistance provides support for business (domestic and foreign owned) proposing new investment in Assisted Areas which creates or safeguards jobs. By encouraging projects which bring new skills and resources to the UK, it can enhance national competitiveness. The Government will give additional emphasis to upgrading skills and technology when allocating funds;

- Industry departments will ensure that RSA negotiations with companies are conducted in a user-friendly way;

Finding new investors

- in an extension of existing activities in North America and Japan, DTI and other departments with industry sponsor responsibilities will identify overseas companies with the potential to invest in the UK;

- Industry departments will give more effective help to investors to find sources of components;

- the Home Office will introduce a new investor category in the Immigration Rules;

Overseas promotion

- private sector secondees will be recruited and there will be greater interchange between IBB and FCO staff;

Regional issues

- RDOs will be encouraged to benchmark the "product" they offer the investor;

- in England, the Government Regional Offices will concentrate on the needs of investors, including infrastructure provision, and overcoming planning delays. They will encourage and assist all regional interests to work together to ensure that the investor is presented with a single approach; and

Sites

- IBB will establish a national and regional strategic site bank with English Partnerships alongside the existing arrangements in Scotland, Wales and Northern Ireland.

Outward Investment

8.60 The Government will:

- encourage its Export Promoters (businessmen on secondment) to look for investment opportunities in the markets for which they are responsible;

- ensure that the Overseas Trade Service's Country Market Plans highlight the potential for investment, and draw relevant opportunities (and risks) to the attention of potential investors;

- expand the network of double taxation treaties, and modernise existing ones, to minimise tax barriers on UK overseas trade and investment;

- review ECGD's Overseas Investment Insurance Scheme and evaluate carefully the Overseas Investment Enquiry Service and Strategic Alliance Service, to see if there are lessons for other markets; and

- commission a study of outward investment to consider what further support the Government might offer UK overseas investors.

FINANCE FOR BUSINESS

9.1 Investment is essential for wealth creation. It depends on many factors. A stable economic background is the most important. Low inflation and low interest rates are crucial. CBI industrial surveys consistently point to anticipated future demand and profitability being more important than the supply of funds. But businesses do need capital to grow. The availability of finance is therefore a vital issue.

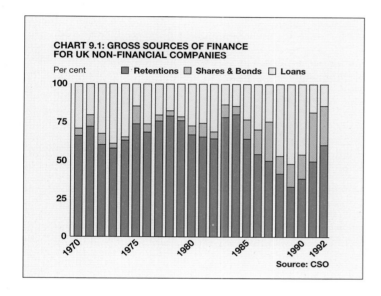

CHART 9.1: GROSS SOURCES OF FINANCE FOR UK NON-FINANCIAL COMPANIES

Per cent ■ Retentions ■ Shares & Bonds □ Loans

Source: CSO

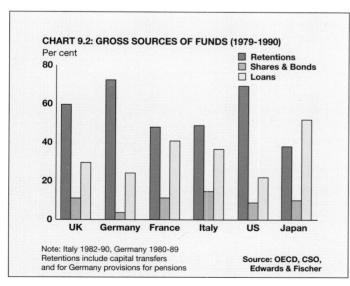

CHART 9.2: GROSS SOURCES OF FUNDS (1979-1990)

Per cent ■ Retentions ■ Shares & Bonds □ Loans

UK   Germany   France   Italy   US   Japan

Note: Italy 1982-90, Germany 1980-89
Retentions include capital transfers and for Germany provisions for pensions

Source: OECD, CSO, Edwards & Fischer

The UK system

9.2 Although many large UK companies rely on domestic financial markets to a considerable extent, they can also gain access to finance from all over the world. However, a significant proportion of total UK employment, as in other G7 countries, is in small and medium sized enterprises (SMEs). The effectiveness of our domestic financial institutions in supplying funds to all sizes of firms is therefore vital.

9.3 Retained earnings are by far the largest source of funds for non-financial companies in the UK. Borrowing is the next most important (chart 9.1). Funds raised by new issues tend to be balanced out by purchases of equities by companies, for example, in takeovers. Smaller unquoted firms may rely still more heavily on retained earnings.

9.4 International comparisons show that:

- other countries share the UK business sector's reliance on retained earnings as the main source of funds (chart 9.2);

- there is a greater reliance on overdrafts in the UK. A Bank of England report[1] shows overdrafts account for 56 per cent of small firm debt in the UK compared to 14 per cent in Germany;

[1] *Finance for Small Firms.* [Bank of England] (1994)

- life assurance and pension funds own a much larger proportion of shares in the UK than in other countries (chart 9.3); and

- the total amount of venture capital invested in the UK is more than twice the level in any other European country. However, investments in the UK tend to be in management buy-outs and the provision of development, rather than start-up, capital. This can place new, higher risk businesses at a disadvantage.

9.5 The UK financial system shares a number of features with those in the US and in other English speaking countries, but differs from that elsewhere in Europe and the Far East. The UK and US have been described as having "outsider" systems because of the importance of open equity markets under which companies are owned by a large group of unconnected institutions and persons. This contrasts with the "insider" system of continental Europe where many fewer companies are quoted, industrial cross shareholding is common, and contested takeovers are rarer.

9.6 However, not all the features of the US market exist in the UK. In particular, institutional investors hold a much greater proportion of UK equities than in the US.

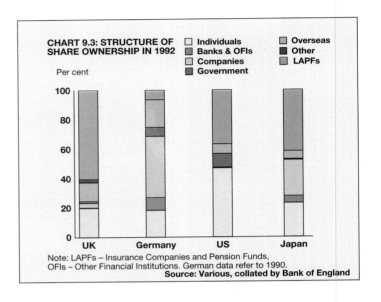

CHART 9.3: STRUCTURE OF SHARE OWNERSHIP IN 1992

Per cent

Legend: Individuals, Banks & OFIs, Companies, Government, Overseas, Other, LAPFs

Note: LAPFs – Insurance Companies and Pension Funds, OFIs – Other Financial Institutions. German data refer to 1990.
Source: Various, collated by Bank of England

Areas of concern

9.7 The UK financial system is amongst the world's most sophisticated. However, there have been expressions of concern over the supply of finance to industry. These concerns are summarised below.

Dividend payout ratios

9.8 Following a rapid rise in the late 1980s, UK companies now tend to distribute a relatively high proportion of their profits in dividends (chart 9.4). This is broadly similar to the US but above that in Germany and Japan. French levels of distribution were higher for most of the 1980s,

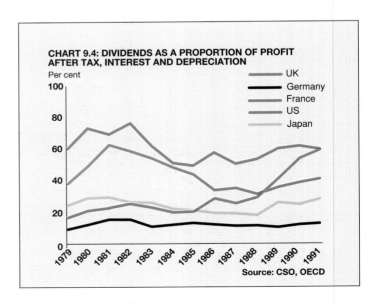

CHART 9.4: DIVIDENDS AS A PROPORTION OF PROFIT AFTER TAX, INTEREST AND DEPRECIATION

Per cent

Legend: UK, Germany, France, US, Japan

Source: CSO, OECD

but are now lower. The issue may not be so much one of the level of dividend payments, as with their apparent inflexibility in response to different trading conditions. This can result in the cost of servicing equity becoming a fixed element, like the cost of debt.

9.9 The policy of making and maintaining cash distributions is sometimes thought to reduce the flow of funds for investment. More generally it may reinforce a pressure on management to show good returns in the short term, even though this may be at the expense of long term growth.

9.10 Pressure on management to improve performance is desirable. So pressure for high dividends is not of itself evidence of a malfunction in the market. Funds distributed as dividends may be recycled and made available for investment. The key issue is whether capital is best allocated by being left in the hands of companies or by being returned to shareholders.

Reliance on overdraft finance

9.11 Overdrafts are often quicker and cheaper to arrange than term loans and the business only has to pay interest on the funds it uses. However, many businesses do not expect overdrafts to be withdrawn and come to rely on them as permanent sources of finance. This can give rise to misunderstanding and resentment when a bank wishes to reduce its exposure. There is evidence that both banks and businesses are now beginning to place greater weight on longer term finance.

Range of financial instruments

9.12 SMEs have traditionally relied heavily on overdrafts. While they offer the advantage of flexibility, and are often frequently attractively priced, they were not intended to form core capital. However, in recent years banks have extended their range of products to include fixed rate loans, term loans and factoring services in greater volume. These types of finance complement overdrafts.

Relations between banks and small businesses

9.13 Many owners of small businesses have criticised banks for placing too much emphasis on security. This can be a particular problem in arranging medium to long-term finance for small businesses, especially in innovative, high technology areas. SMEs also complain that the full benefit of interest rate reductions are not passed on and that charges levied by banks are not commensurate with the level of risk. However, successive reviews by the Bank of England and the Treasury have confirmed the commitment of the banks to small businesses. And in November 1992 the Bank found that although margins had widened on around a third of all accounts, they had narrowed on one account in ten and were unchanged on the remainder.

Late Payment

9.14 There has long been recognition that the late payment of commercial debt is a serious problem for small businesses. Most other countries also suffer from late payment. The position in the UK is improving and payment times are now a little better than the average for the EC. But the problem remains a significant one. In November 1993, DTI sought views on how to address the problem, including legislation for a statutory right to interest.

What the Bank of England and the Government have done

9.15 As indicated above, the Bank and the Government have examined the relations between banks and SMEs on a number of occasions, most recently in 1993. As a result:

- codes of practice for banks' small business customers have been issued by all the major banks;

- with the Government's encouragement, the powers of the Banking Ombudsman have been extended; and

- banks have been encouraged to provide a wider range of products.

9.16 The **Small Firms Loan Guarantee Scheme (SFLGS)** was introduced in 1981 to promote investment when conventional loans were not available due to lack of security or proven track record. From July 1993, premiums have been reduced to ½ per cent for guarantees on fixed rate lending, and to 1½ per cent for guarantees on variable rate lending. The maximum size of loan available to established businesses has been increased from £100,000 to £250,000 while the guaranteed proportion has been increased from 70 to 85 per cent. Since the improvements were introduced, the number of loans guaranteed each month has doubled.

9.17 In the November 1993 Budget, the Government introduced a new **Enterprise Investment Scheme (EIS)** to replace the Business Expansion Scheme. In March 1994 it issued a consultation document[2] to seek views on a new **Venture Capital Trust (VCT)** scheme. An important feature of the EIS is that investors may become paid directors. This will encourage 'business angels' who want to invest in companies as

[2]*Venture Capital Trusts: A Consultative Document.* [Inland Revenue] (1994)

well as contribute their expertise. VCTs will permit pooled investments in unquoted trading companies. Investors will receive dividends and capital gains tax free. Changes to capital gains tax reliefs will help to encourage investment in unquoted companies.

IMPROVING THE COMPETITIVENESS OF THE FINANCIAL SERVICES SECTOR

The completion of the Single Market in financial services has offered opportunities for UK businesses to expand their operations across Europe.

The Government and the Bank have taken a number of measures recently to improve competitiveness in this sector:
- *the simplified tax treatment of foreign exchange gains and losses will bring the UK more closely into line with its competitors*
- *a new and simple tax regime for financial instruments such as swaps, derivatives and currency contracts will help in managing interest rates and currency risk*
- *Open Ended Investment Companies (OEICs) should help UK firms compete with foreign funds selling into the UK, and help UK funds sell abroad. The Government hopes to have new powers in force during 1995 under the European Communities Act*
- *a new securities settlement system (CREST) for London has been specified by a team led by the Bank*

New Initiatives

9.18 The Treasury is looking at the whole area of the supply of finance under its industrial finance initiative. This work covers:

- capital markets, savings generally, and the flow of funds to business; and

- implications for taxation and other policies.

9.19 As part of this work, Treasury Ministers have sought the views of business throughout the UK, including a large number of representatives of SMEs. Although this work is ongoing, the Government believes that there are some initiatives that it and the private sector can take now.

Improving corporate governance

9.20 The Government welcomes the steps being taken by the Accounting Standards Board (ASB) to improve company reporting. In particular, it welcomes:

- the debate on acquisition accounting practices, following the publication of the draft standard on fair values in acquisition accounting and a discussion paper on goodwill and intangible assets. Current UK accounting practice may favour companies which grow by acquisition rather than organically;

- the standard on reporting financial performance which provides a framework to encourage investors to analyse financial statements more fully;

- the standard on reporting the substance of transactions. This requires companies to report the substance of a transaction, rather than the legal form of its parts; and

- the operating and financial review which sets out the best practice on communicating with shareholders.

9.21 Some recent pay awards to some senior executives of UK companies have been of concern to many. Shareholders may have inadequate information to judge whether directors have earned their remuneration. The Government believes that pay must be shown to respond to market conditions in both directions.

9.22 The Cadbury Committee has encouraged companies to provide full and clear disclosure of directors' remuneration. The Committee is monitoring the position and expects the subject to be on the agenda of its successor body when it is appointed next year.

9.23 The independence of auditors is essential if investors are to obtain reliable information on financial performance. The professional bodies have taken steps to ensure that this independence is maintained. The Government will continue to watch this area carefully.

Encouraging the supply of long term finance

9.24 A stable, long term relationship between investors and company management brings many benefits. Such relationships depend on communication and understanding. The private sector bears the main responsibility for developing such relationships. However, the Government can act as a catalyst. For example, the Government:

- co-funded "Engineering Consensus Good Disclosure Practice Code"[3];

- has published "Finance for Technology-Based Businesses"[4], endorsed by the CBI and the Bank of England; and

- is acting as facilitator for the private-sector led working group on co-operation between corporate management and institutional shareholders as a stimulus for long term investment and development. The emphasis will be on practical outcomes, such as codes of practice.

[3] Sciteb Ltd. *Engineering Consensus - an industry/city dialogue. Good Disclosure Practice Code.* [Sciteb Ltd] (1993)

[4] Segal Quince Wicksteed Ltd; *Finance for Technology – Based Businesses: A practical guide to getting the right financial support.* [DTI] (1994)

Encouraging the supply of capital to SMEs

9.25 The Government recognises the importance of 'business angels' in providing informal investment to small companies. DTI has supported the development of informal investment by funding a number of TECs to run demonstration projects, in partnership with other local agencies. These bring together potential investors and businesses seeking finance.

- DTI will work with the private sector, Business Links and TECs to raise awareness of this type of investment and develop national coverage of a local brokerage service throughout England. In Scotland the Enterprise networks already provide similar services.

9.26 UK institutional investors place a much higher proportion of their funds in listed equities than their foreign counterparts. They tend to favour easily tradeable, low risk investments with predictable yields. Such tendencies may be reinforced by regulatory requirements for the protection of investors, pensioners and policy holders. Together these factors may inhibit investment in unquoted, risky, but potentially high growth businesses:

- DTI is re-examining the regulatory requirements on insurance companies for the valuation of non-listed securities as part of the deregulation initiative.

9.27 In addition, the Government:

- has introduced a pilot advice and counselling scheme to help borrowers under the SFLGS. The aim is to identify by the end of the three year pilot period whether and how the provision of appropriate advice and counselling can improve the survival rate of SFLGS borrowers;

- recognises that Business Links also have a role to play in helping SMEs identify and access appropriate forms of finance;

- welcomes the Stock Exchange's new listing rules for scientific research based companies, mainly in the field of pharmaceuticals and diagnostics. The Stock Exchange has set up a working group to explore ways of developing these rules further. The Stock Exchange is also considering ways of encouraging the trading of shares in smaller companies; and

- will be seeking an appropriate legislative opportunity to take further the powers on OEICs discussed above.

Tackling Late Payment

9.28 In response to DTI's consultations, strong views were expressed both for and against legislation on a statutory right to interest on late payment. Overall there was a narrow margin in favour of legislation, but there was much concern about the negative impact that it might have on small businesses and no clear mandate from the business community in favour.

9.29 In the light of this the Government has decided not to introduce legislation at this stage. The major need is to bring about a change in business culture and hence shorter payment times. There is no single solution to late payment. The public sector must give a lead. The Government will:

- require all Government departments and their agencies to comply with the CBI prompt payment code;

- require all Government departments and their agencies in their annual reports to set out their payment policies and to state whether they observed the principles of the CBI code;

- require all Government departments and their agencies to publicise their arrangements for handling complaints about failure to pay on time; and

- expect all other public sector bodies to follow central Government's lead.

9.30 The Government will also introduce a package of additional measures including:

- working with the business community to develop further the proposal for a British Standard for prompt payment;

- implementation of proposals to require public companies to state their payment policies in their directors' reports;

- further changes to streamline and simplify court procedures for debt recovery;

- review of court systems with a view to increasing the scope of the informal small claims procedure; and

- work with Business Links, Trade Associations and others to help small businesses to improve their arrangements for credit management and securing payment of debts owed to them.

9.31 The Government will continue to keep the position under review. If there has not been a significant improvement within the next two years it will review the case for legislation.

COMMUNICATIONS AND INFRASTRUCTURE

10.1 Industry depends on good communications. Business people need to make contacts, and to stay in touch when they are travelling. They expect to use the same modern telecommunications and computer equipment at home and abroad. They are as impatient with communications barriers as they are with trade barriers.

10.2 New forms of communications have a profound effect on industry. The canals, the railways and motorways all in turn revolutionised industry and commerce. Today we are experiencing another communications revolution. Demands for new products and services are burgeoning. The once separate worlds of information technology, telecommunications and broadcasting are converging as companies launch information and entertainment services based on the new technologies.

10.3 The range of technologies is expanding rapidly. Their application offers the prospect of vast increases in productivity, and an enormous expansion of choice for consumers. The world demand for them offers a huge potential market. Our service providers - the UK's broadcasters, programme makers, computer programmers, information services providers - now have the chance of selling their services anywhere in the world. Everywhere telecommunications, computer and media companies are jockeying to establish themselves as global players. What can the Government do to help?

COMMUNICATIONS AND BROADCASTING

Telecommunications

10.4 Telecommunications is increasingly key to innovation and efficiency, not only in research and development, but to all phases of production and marketing. It offers major opportunities for growth and employment, particularly for small and medium sized firms and in the knowledge-based industries.

10.5 The pace of technological change in coming years will be dramatic. New developments will spread rapidly around the globe. UK companies must continue to benefit from the widest range of high quality services at competitive prices. Starting in 1984, the Government has liberalised the supply of apparatus and services, privatised BT, and encouraged the development of effective competition in all segments of the market. Ten years later, these once-revolutionary steps are now being considered by many other Governments worldwide. DTI is working to encourage this in order to bring down prices and improve market access throughout the world.

10.6 The investment required to deliver the benefits of technical advances to users is substantial. The UK is up with the best of its international competitors in the construction of these competing high capacity networks. This will not only assist businesses at home, but could also open up important markets overseas for UK companies which have developed new services ahead of their overseas rivals.

10.7 These services will not be limited to the established ones like telephone and fax. They will include public services like education and training. They will bring benefits for particular sectors - like the NHS - and for business as a whole - like home-working and video-conferencing. They will include services now delivered into the home by other means - like games and entertainment - or hardly at all - like banking and shopping. No-one knows just how far and how fast these new services will change our lives, but the Government aims to ensure that the infrastructure is there to meet commercial demands as they emerge.

10.8 A recent study[1] commissioned by DTI concluded that our telecommunications infrastructure, the pace of its development and the range of services available to users all compare well with our major competitors. The industry is currently investing some £4 billion a year. This has been to good effect (chart 10.1). BT and Mercury have wholly fibre optic trunk networks. The cable television companies are taking optical fibre even closer to the customer. The UK's mobile telecommunications industry is one of the largest in the world. We have four national cellular operators, two with services covering more than 90 per cent of the population. Prices have fallen by more than 30 per cent in real terms since BT was privatised in 1984.

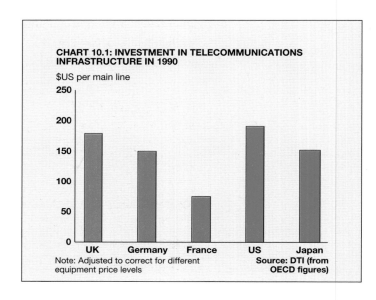

CHART 10.1: INVESTMENT IN TELECOMMUNICATIONS INFRASTRUCTURE IN 1990

$US per main line

Note: Adjusted to correct for different equipment price levels

Source: DTI (from OECD figures)

10.9 The 1991 White Paper on Telecommunications policy[2] introduced more liberal arrangements for licensing networks. The Government remains committed to the White Paper policies, and in particular to the importance of securing the development of competing telecommunications infrastructure. Since 1991, around 80 applications for new telecommunications licences have been received, and over 40 issued. Thirteen of the new licence-holders are planning their own public networks to compete with BT and Mercury. Improving the arrangements for interconnection of these networks is a high priority. It will be particularly important to give the widest

[1]PA Consulting Group: *Study of the International Competitiveness of the UK Telecommunications Infrastructure.* [DTI] (1994)

[2]*Competition and Choice: Telecommunications policy for the 1990s.* Cm 1461 [HMSO] (1991)

range of customers access to the new high-capacity networks and to ensure the networks are easily available to all those with services to provide over them.

10.10 The Government wants UK manufacturers to take maximum advantage of investment in this infrastructure. This requires close dialogue and partnership between UK manufacturers on the one hand, and BT and the newer telecom operators, including the cable TV franchisees, on the other. The Government is examining further initiatives with both manufacturers and telecommunications operators aimed at improving performance.

10.11 The EC has set a target of 1 January 1998 for the liberalisation of voice telephony services. While welcoming this, the UK wants faster progress. This is essential to the implementation of Europe-wide telecommunications networks. But while UK telecommunications remain in advance of the rest of the EC, this will attract international firms to the UK and to the City of London in particular.

Broadcasting

10.12 The market for broadcasting is also undergoing rapid and far-reaching change. The introduction of digital techniques will greatly increase the capacity of broadcasting systems to deliver services. Barriers between broadcasting, telecommunications and computing are coming down. New services are being developed and demanded. The limits to competition set by the scarcity of frequencies for terrestrial broadcasting are being eroded by the introduction of cable and satellite broadcasting systems, and the greater efficiency in the use of frequencies which will be obtained through digital technology.

10.13 We have key assets in the quality and creativeness of UK programme makers - the BBC, the ITV companies, and over 800 independent production companies. The rapidly expanding cable and satellite systems now serve over 800,000 (of which almost 650,000 are the more modern broadband systems) and over 2½ million UK households respectively. Many new services tend to rely initially on low cost programming from the United States. However the UK is the world's second largest exporter of television programmes, with 8 to 9 per cent of world markets. Opportunities exist for the UK industry to do more overseas.

10.14 The industry's competitiveness is largely in its own hands. But the Government can play a part. There are three areas where Government policy can have most effect:

- **the future of the BBC.** The performance of the BBC in international markets is vital. It already accounts for half of our programme exports and should build on this to take full advantage of expanding global markets. The Government will recognise this in its proposals for the future of the BBC which will be published shortly;

- **media ownership restrictions.** The Government is reviewing the restrictions on ownership of broadcasting and newspaper companies. It is considering whether they strike the right balance between promoting choice for the consumer, and the interest of the industry in playing an active part in international markets; and

- **support for equipment producers.** The Government headed off plans by the EC to lock Europe into obsolete analogue-based High Definition Television. Instead, it has helped to establish a new European forum to promote the launch of digital video broadcasting. The associated demands for equipment will give our manufacturers the incentive to provide new receiving equipment and for an early entry into world markets.

DIGITAL VIDEO BROADCASTING

Digital technology is already transforming TV studios and is expected to reach many viewers over the coming decade:

- *it is likely to offer viewers more channels, better pictures, mobile TV and the merging of entertainment and business applications*
- *the UK network and consumer digital TV equipment market will be worth £5 billion to £10 billion over 15 years and considerably more world wide*
- *it could eventually release radio spectrum worth £5 billion a year to UK business*

The UK can capture a significant share of this market. It has a strong base of Far East inward investors, leading to the UK becoming a net exporter of TV sets, and some go-ahead indigenous companies. But Governments in competitor countries are developing strategies to bring digital video broadcasting to their markets. The best chance for UK based companies will come with the UK market moving ahead with the fastest of our competitors, whether by satellite, cable or terrestrial means.

The Government has a particular role in the terrestrial means through its control of radio frequencies. Digital technology is far more efficient than analogue technology. If there is a firm commitment from broadcasters to introduce digital terrestrial television services at an early date, the Government would be prepared to give priority to frequency channels for digital technology over analogue technology. This would secure the advantages of digital technology as rapidly as possible.

Radio Spectrum

10.15 The radio spectrum is a vital, but limited, resource. Many success stories of the last decade, such as the explosive growth in the use of mobile telephones and the expansion of independent local and national radio broadcasting have hinged on access to spectrum. New developments such as the use of radio for the local delivery of telecommunications, the delivery of advanced data and multimedia services to mobile terminals, and microwave video distribution systems to deliver a plethora of television services are all contending for access to the spectrum.

10.16 This demand for frequencies is outstripping the pace of technological change in expanding the accessible spectrum. Proper management is essential if shortage of frequencies is not to become a barrier to growth. Much has been done by DTI's Radiocommunications Agency. The rolling review of Government departments' use of spectrum will result in further release and sharing of frequencies. MoD will pursue, in consultation with our NATO allies, the release of spectrum for use by the emergency services. This would in turn release key UHF spectrum for commercial users.

10.17 More fundamental changes are also being considered. DTI's recent consultative document[3] sets out options for more efficient management of the spectrum. These include a greater role for commercial organisations to plan and license radio use, and more use of the price mechanism.

Posts

10.18 The Post Office provides a communication and distribution network serving 24½ million addresses, including 1 million business premises. Around 90 per cent of the Post Office's annual turnover of £4½ billion for letters and parcels stems from traffic to, or from, businesses. Since 1981, when the Government reduced the postal monopoly to its present level of £1, a private sector courier industry has developed providing value-added premium services, and generating revenues of £200 million per year.

10.19 The UK's postal service compares well in terms of value for money and quality of service with those of our EC and other major trading partners. The President of the Board of Trade is conducting a review of the Post Office and the Trade and Industry Select Committee has itself recently completed a report[4]. The Government will respond to the Select Committee when its review is complete.

[3]Radiocommunications Agency; *The Future Management of the Radio Spectrum* [DTI] (1994)

[4]Trade and Industry Select Committee; *First Report on Future of the Post Office* HC 207 [HMSO] (1994)

TRANSPORT

10.20 Transport is an unavoidable part of the cost structure of almost every business and of the UK economy as a whole. Businesses need to get their supplies in, their products out to market, and their employees to and from work. The speed and reliability of transport affect business costs and investment decisions. Congestion, accidents and excessive freight and travel costs lead to greater cost burdens on businesses, higher prices and lost markets. A high-quality, efficiently priced transport infrastructure can also attract international businesses and tourists, and contribute to regional development. A new report[5] by KPMG Peat Marwick, who interviewed senior executives of foreign companies operating in the UK, found that "the UK's infrastructure and transport were highly rated with closeness to key markets, roads, air and rail access all exceeding expectations".

10.21 In the past, some of our major competitors have spent a greater proportion of their national income on transport infrastructure than we have. However, more recently expenditure on transport in the UK has been increased significantly (chart 10.2). Over the next three years, total public sector spending on investment for transport is planned to total £14 billion.

10.22 Simplistic comparisons of expenditure can be misleading. Transport investment decisions are determined by a number of factors, including physical geography and the size and distribution of population. For example, the UK has a much higher population density than many EC countries. This affects demand for particular types of infrastructure (such as inter urban motorways and bypasses which reduce congestion and take heavy traffic away from our towns and villages) and means that we have to give greater consideration to environmental factors. The fact that Great Britain is a relatively small island makes freight transport by road more attractive than rail, but increases the potential for aviation and shipping for international freight and passenger movements.

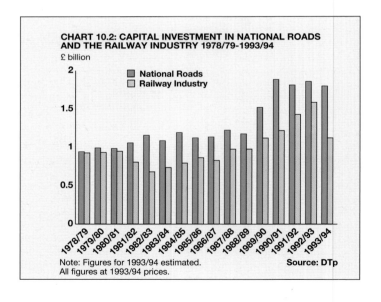

CHART 10.2: CAPITAL INVESTMENT IN NATIONAL ROADS AND THE RAILWAY INDUSTRY 1978/79-1993/94

Note: Figures for 1993/94 estimated. All figures at 1993/94 prices.

Source: DTp

[5] *A Survey of Foreign Owned Companies in the UK.* [KPMG Peat Marwick] (1994)

The Government's Approach

10.23 Economic assessment has long been a key element in transport investment decisions, reflecting the important but complex links between infrastructure investment and economic activity. There has also been increasing awareness in recent years of the wider costs imposed by transport, especially those on the environment. The Government's approach is that transport decisions should both address transport needs and preserve or enhance the environment. The UK Sustainable Development Strategy[6] therefore committed the Government to further work to improve understanding of these different costs and benefits, the way they are taken into account in investment decisions, and the underlying relationships.

10.24 Against this economic and environmental background the Government has set a framework within which adequate and appropriate infrastructure can continue to be developed, maintained safely and operated efficiently and effectively. There are six main elements:

- using the skills and resources of the private sector to the maximum extent possible;

- fostering competition and choice;

- continuing structural investment and support for transport infrastructure, and for socially necessary services;

- employing price mechanisms which make users aware of the full costs of travel, including the environmental costs;

- appropriate regulation; and

- providing for economic and social needs for access with less need for travel.

10.25 The achievements of privatisation were set out in chapter 1. Privatisation has been a major success in the transport sector. Our industries are now competing more effectively and with far fewer constraints than before in both domestic and international markets. The PFI is fast becoming a cornerstone of transport policy.

---

[6] *Sustainable Development - the UK strategy.* Cm 2426 [HMSO] (1994)

PRIVATISATION IN THE TRANSPORT SECTOR

A number of major businesses has been privatised since 1979:

- *National Freight Corporation was sold to its employees in 1982, and is now the second largest company in the sector*
- *the sale of 72 subsidiaries of the National Bus Company and ten subsidiaries of the Scottish Bus Group were key elements in bus deregulation. 28 local authority bus companies have also been sold. Vehicle mileage has been increased, operating costs and subsidy reduced*
- *British Airways is the world's largest international passenger airline*
- *BAA's success has set the example for the privatisation of local authority owned airports, and is leading to significant new investment and expansion abroad*
- *privatisation is revitalising the former Trust Ports of Tees and Hartlepool, Tilbury, Medway, Clyde and the Forth*
- *the successors to the British Transport Docks Board and Sealink are now substantial private sector companies*

More recently the Government has started to privatise and liberalise British Rail. This will make the railway more responsive to the needs of general and business users. It will open up new commercial opportunities in the operation of passenger and freight services and in the provision of infrastructure and rolling stock. Businesses which enter these new markets will be well placed to take advantage of increasing opportunities in other countries.

Privatisation has led to significantly improved efficiency, reductions in costs and substantial increases in investment. Businesses which were previously held back by public sector constraints have become major players in international markets.

Further privatisation measures planned or under consideration include:

- *the CAA's air traffic control operations*
- *more Trust Ports*
- *Belfast Airport*
- *local authority owned airports*
- *the remaining local authority owned bus companies and subsidiaries of London Buses Ltd*

Roads

10.26 Every business in the country relies to some extent on the road network. Around 90 per cent of surface freight travels by road.

10.27 The Government has an excellent record of investment in delivering the increased motorway and trunk road capacity which is so vital to the economic well-being of the country. Capital investment in roads is now 87 per cent higher than in 1978/79. Between 1994/95 and 1996/97, the Government plans public expenditure on national and local roads of around £3 billion a year. The UK has increased the proportion of national income spent on roads (chart 10.3).

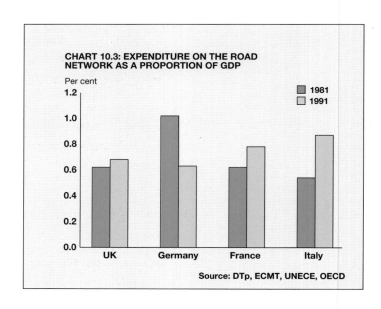

CHART 10.3: EXPENDITURE ON THE ROAD NETWORK AS A PROPORTION OF GDP

Source: DTp, ECMT, UNECE, OECD

10.28 Improving the road network is not just a matter of building more and more roads; spending substantial amounts of public money; or even increasing the contribution from private finance. Apart from the limitations on resources, there are physical constraints and environmental issues to be considered.

10.29 The efficiency with which roads are used is also important, since this can have a significant effect on demand. An essential part of this is to provide a market under which users and investors are faced with appropriate pricing signals. This is particularly important in roads, where users do not pay directly, but through the tax system. Direct charging could reduce congestion by providing another source of finance to improve the network more quickly and, by encouraging its more efficient use, provide significant benefits to industry. The Government is developing motorway tolling. It is also researching congestion charging in urban areas, where it is often much more difficult to increase road capacity.

10.30 Electronic motorway tolling will sharply increase the scope for involving private finance and management skills. Tolling could be introduced by 1998. In the meantime, in order to give the private sector further practical experience of designing, building, financing and operating roads, the Government will let some contracts in which it will pay the toll per vehicle rather than levying a charge on the user.

10.31 The Government has introduced a package of measures to speed up delivery of the most important improvements in the trunk road programme to make journeys run more smoothly, minimising blight, damage and disruption for local communities and the environment. The main elements are:

- a review of priorities, based on a number of criteria, including the costs/benefits, the contribution to the efficiency and competitiveness of the economy, and the need to achieve a proper balance between the needs of individuals, industry and the environment;

- the decisions announced at the end of March will ensure that the most urgently needed and important schemes are dealt with first and delivered more quickly, and will avoid wasteful preliminary expenditure on lower priority schemes;

- the setting up of an executive agency - The Highways Agency - charged with delivering the trunk road programme by the most cost-effective and efficient means;

- changes in the Highways Inquiry Procedure Rules to speed up proceedings and make them more efficient without diminishing people's rights of objection; and

- trials of pre-inquiry planning conferences designed to involve the public earlier and promote a less adversarial approach.

10.32 In Scotland, the Scottish Office is focusing investment on a core network of strategic routes of greatest concern to commerce and industry. In Northern Ireland, priority is being given to upgrading the main inter-urban roads, especially those to the main ports and airports.

10.33 In Wales, priority for major improvements to the trunk road network will be concentrated on the A55 across North Wales, the M4 across South Wales, and the A465 'Heads of the Valleys' road. These are key routes which provide access to domestic and international markets, and which underpin the competitiveness of the Welsh economy.

TRANSPORT AND DEVELOPMENTS IN INFORMATION TECHNOLOGY

There are exciting opportunities for new technology in the transport sector:
- *the infrastructure and in-vehicle equipment needed for road pricing is a huge business opportunity*
- *a UK invention is able to bring drivers up-to-date advice about motorway congestion by taking advantage of existing telecommunications infrastructure*
- *important opportunities exist to build on the success of speed cameras with automatic video-based equipment*
- *developments in information handling, telecommunications and satellite navigation promise an increase in the effective capacity of the air space to meet forecast growth in demand for air travel well into the next century*
- *these technologies will also benefit the marine and rail sectors, and assist inter-modal transport*
- *growth in teleworking and videoconferencing could reduce the demand for transport*

Rail

10.34 The amount of freight carried on the railways has been declining for a long period, although rail remains the principal mode for the carriage of bulky products such as coal, steel and iron. Rail systems carry significant numbers of commuters and other business travellers. In 1990, for example, British Rail (BR) and London Underground provided a total of 475 million commuting and 67 million business journeys.

10.35 Capital investment on the railways has risen significantly in real terms in since 1983. Capital investment in the London Underground has also significantly increased.

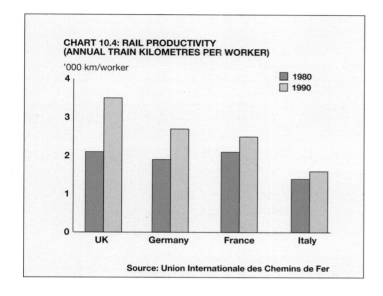

CHART 10.4: RAIL PRODUCTIVITY (ANNUAL TRAIN KILOMETRES PER WORKER)

'000 km/worker

☐ 1980
☐ 1990

Source: Union Internationale des Chemins de Fer

10.36 BR has made substantial improvements in efficiency in recent years: its productivity is significantly higher than in France, Germany or Italy (chart 10.4). BR and London Transport also operate at low levels of subsidy by international standards and so make fewer demands on the taxpayer than many other countries' railway systems.

10.37 BR privatisation and liberalisation will bring considerable benefits to industry and the travelling public. The first six passenger train operating companies will be franchised in 1995. The quality of services has already been improved following the introduction of Passenger's Charters. Private ownership and competition should reduce operating costs through improved efficiency. Railtrack will also have major incentives to bear down on costs. This may help to stem the flow of freight away from rail and on to road, and open up new markets, especially following the start of Channel Tunnel services. In order to ease the transition period, to ensure that rail freight has a fair chance to compete, and to achieve environmental benefits the Government has enhanced rail freight grants.

10.38 Light rail systems offer a clean and efficient means of cutting down on congestion and pollution within cities. A number of schemes is being developed. These include the South Yorkshire "Supertram", which is receiving significant financial assistance from the Government.

10.39 The PFI is harnessing the skills and resources of the private sector in further developing the rail sector. The Channel Tunnel is a major piece of new infrastructure constructed without any support from the taxpayer. The Heathrow Express is being taken forward mainly by the private sector. The Jubilee Line extension has a significant contribution from the private sector. Major candidates for joint ventures between the private and public sector include the Second Channel Tunnel Rail Link, Crossrail and the modernisation of the West Coast Main Line. A competition is being launched for new privately financed trains for London Underground's Northern Line.

> ### TRANSPORT IN TOWNS AND CITIES
>
> *Most businesses are in towns and cities; and a huge proportion of all journeys start or finish there:*
>
> - *many cities suffer badly from congestion, increasing costs to business*
> - *cities that are environmentally attractive are better places to live in; this can help draw in more business investment*
> - *businesses in towns are sometimes concerned about the effects of traffic restraint schemes on trade. But there is often popular demand for traffic control; and well designed schemes can attract business*
> - *there is less scope for building new roads in cities. But there are many more opportunities for using public transport*
> - *new transport links can help regenerate run down inner cities*
>
> *The Government is taking a number of initiatives:*
>
> - *helping to fund major **public transport investment** in cities, including private finance wherever possible. Schemes include light rail projects in Manchester and Sheffield; and improved links to Docklands*
> - ***new planning guidance** to promote new development in towns and cities in places which people can reach without having to use cars*
> - *encouraging local authorities to **propose local transport strategies** and investment covering both public and private transport (known as "the package approach")*
> - ***speeding up buses**, through bus priority measures and 'red routes'*
> - *improving transport in **run down inner city areas**. Examples are: new 'spine roads' in the Black Country and Bristol; improved rail and canal links at Trafford Park in Manchester; and a new central bus station in Liverpool*
> - *looking for new ways of **tackling congestion**. A number of cities is looking at new means of reducing the effects of traffic while ensuring that business in the city centres flourish. The Government is sponsoring the biggest research project ever into vehicle congestion charging, to see whether it has a contribution to make, especially in London*

Buses and Coaches

10.40 Most local bus services have been privatised and deregulated. This has led to an increase of 21 per cent in vehicle mileage outside London and a reduction in operator costs by about a third. Over 80 per cent of bus mileage is now being operated without subsidy, which has been reduced by about a half in real terms. But buses are increasingly impeded by traffic congestion and the Government is encouraging local authorities to give greater priority for buses in traffic management schemes. Deregulation has also improved the competitiveness of long-distance coach services, in competition with cars and the railways. More services are being provided, with a resulting increase in passengers.

Aviation

10.41 Air transport has expanded enormously over the last 30 years. Journeys have trebled, and passengers increased almost sevenfold. Good air links are essential to firms which compete in international markets, and play an important part in attracting inward investment.

10.42 The industry is also an important component of the UK economy in its own right. Over 100,000 people are employed at our airports and by our airlines.

Expenditure by air travellers visiting the UK and by foreign travellers on UK airlines amounts to over £9 billion a year. Heathrow is the busiest international airport in the world, handling 48 million passengers in 1993. It has been a powerful economic motor. Good management, the success of UK airlines and the strength of London as a commercial centre have all played a part. Heathrow's success has attracted other industries to West London and the Thames Valley and bred a web of supporting industries. Regional airports are also increasingly important to business.

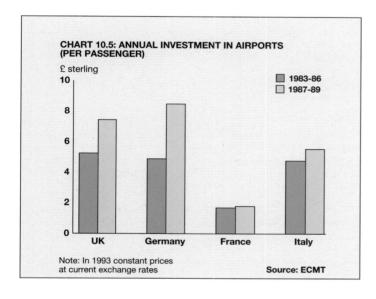

CHART 10.5: ANNUAL INVESTMENT IN AIRPORTS (PER PASSENGER)

£ sterling

- 1983-86
- 1987-89

Note: In 1993 constant prices at current exchange rates

Source: ECMT

10.43 During the 1980s almost all the UK's principal airports, and many of the smaller ones, have benefited from major investment to improve facilities and increase capacity. Within the EC only Germany has invested more per passenger (chart 10.5). Most of this investment has come from the private sector, particularly following the privatisation of BAA.

10.44 International air transport has suffered from over regulation and complex barriers to trade. The UK played a major part in bringing the single European air transport market into effect in 1993. This has widened the range of services and lowered some prices (thanks to the initiatives of UK airlines), although the market needs to develop further and be made to work properly. The Government will continue to press for this. Beyond Europe protectionism remains rife. The Government is continuing to seek the liberalisation of air service arrangements wherever possible. This could have major benefits, including increasing opportunities for tourism.

10.45 Business aviation facilities can increase an area's attractiveness to business. Because of increasing pressure on facilities available for general and business aviation use in the South East, the Government will be seeking views on the scope for developing civil aviation at the MoD airfield at Northolt.

10.46 Following work by the Civil Aviation Authority (CAA) and Government departments, the Government is proposing that the National Air Traffic Services (NATS) should be established as a privatised contractor to the CAA. Privatisation will facilitate the substantial investment needed to ensure that the UK's air traffic control capacity can accommodate forecast air traffic growth, while delivering greater management efficiency. In privatising NATS the Government will ensure that the UK's high safety standards are maintained through continuing regulation by the CAA's

Safety Regulation Group. The Secretary of State for Transport is inviting the views of the aviation community and of other interested parties. The timing of legislation will be dependent on the availability of Parliamentary time.

Ports and Shipping

10.47 Over 95 per cent of UK trade by volume passes through our **ports.** Growth in seaborne trade has been healthy. Only the Netherlands handles more freight. Well over half of the UK's port capacity is now owned by private sector companies. The abolition of the Dock Labour Scheme, and the creation of the framework which permits Trust Ports to privatise themselves, have enabled many ports to modernise their working practices and take advantage of up-to-date cargo handling technology.

10.48 The UK **shipping** industry has contracted sharply over the last 30 years, although it remains an important contributor to the economy. This is not purely a UK problem; the EC fleet as a whole is now less than 50 per cent of its 1980s size, and the Japanese flagged fleet has shrunk to 20 per cent of its 1970s size. The trend in UK owned shipping in recent years has been towards the more sophisticated, high value-added areas of cruise, ferry and containers, where the quality and the technical expertise of the industry can best be exploited to competitive advantage. Structural changes in the industry, the reform of labour relations, and the efforts of individual companies to improve efficiency and reduce costs have helped give it a much more competitive base. The recently announced decision to introduce a provision which will allow capital allowance balancing charges for ships to be rolled over for a period of up to three years from 21 April 1994, will provide further help where tax measures available overseas put some parts of our shipping industry at a particular disadvantage.

10.49 The Government continues to press for liberalisation of shipping services and the containment and eventual elimination of state aids. The requirements of the UK shipping register have been simplified. Within the EC, shipowners can now operate on all international routes to, from and between Member States, and coastal and offshore cabotage services have been opened up. This will help to give a further boost to coastal shipping, which accounts for nearly 20 per cent of total freight movements in the UK.

10.50 The UK has been instrumental in establishing maritime competition rules within the EC. These promote the provision of reasonably priced and efficient shipping services for the benefit of EC traders and consumers, while also recognising the special characteristics of the international shipping industry. The Government will continue to press for arrangements which ensure the long-term stability of the industry, in the interests of shippers and shipowners alike.

10.51 As well as continuing to play a leading role in the International Maritime Organisation, the Government has supported the EC's wide-ranging programme of measures on maritime safety. These aim to eliminate sub-standard shipping from EC waters. Not only will these measures save lives and reduce marine pollution, they will also protect UK shipowners from unfair competition from those operators who do not comply with internationally agreed standards.

OTHER UTILITIES

10.52 All industrial processes and commercial services use energy and water. In some cases they are a large part of total costs, in most they are a relatively minor part. But most firms depend on them for continued production. Efficient and reliable energy and water networks therefore underpin competitiveness.

10.53 The aim of the Government's energy and water policies is to ensure secure and sustainable supplies at competitive prices. The Government believes that this will best be achieved through privatisation, competitive energy markets, and so long as monopolies remain in some areas, a regulatory system which acts as a proxy for the competitive process.

10.54 Even with increased competition in energy generation and supply, it is estimated that there is still the potential to save around 20 per cent of energy consumed in industry through proven technologies and cost effective measures having paybacks of three to five years. The Government's Energy Efficiency Office develops and runs programmes aimed at overcoming market barriers and stimulating increased cost effective investment in energy efficiency.

Electricity Supply

10.55 Electricity is necessary for the operation of most manufacturing processes and for control of virtually all industrial and commercial activities. Industries such as chemicals, engineering, metals, paper and vehicles are large users.

10.56 Average electricity prices paid by industrial consumers are around the middle of the range of prices paid elsewhere, and below prices paid in some of our major competitors, notably Japan and Germany (chart 10.6). However it is suggested that some large consumers elsewhere in the EC may be purchasing electricity on particularly advantageous terms which cannot be matched in the UK on a commercial basis.

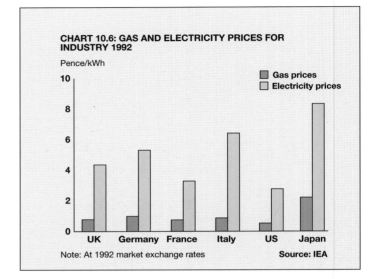

CHART 10.6: GAS AND ELECTRICITY PRICES FOR INDUSTRY 1992

Pence/kWh

Gas prices
Electricity prices

UK   Germany   France   Italy   US   Japan

Note: At 1992 market exchange rates   Source: IEA

10.57 Most of the electricity supply industry has been privatised since 1990. New private sector companies have been created. Several of these have started to play an important role in international markets as contractors, or as members of joint ventures with overseas companies. The UK has developed a new expertise in the provision of private sector energy services to add to its old expertise in energy engineering and project management.

10.58 Competition is reducing costs. With the opening of the market to medium sized customers in April, some 50,000 industrial customers (who account for approximately half the total electricity consumed) are already able to choose their supplier. Many more will be able to do so from April 1998.

10.59 Although the impact on prices varies, the average price paid by industrial electricity consumers fell by about 6½ per cent in real terms between 1989 and 1993, as a result of big reductions in 1990 and 1991. Smaller commercial customers are also benefitting. The public electricity suppliers have either frozen or reduced their basic tariffs in both 1993/94 and 1994/95. As a result, tariff prices have fallen by 7 per cent in real terms since 1992.

10.60 In February, National Power and PowerGen gave undertakings that over the next two years they would seek to sell a total of 6,000 MW of generating plant, and that they would bid prices in the Electricity Pool in a way best calculated to achieve an average pool price of 2.4p/kWh. The undertakings on price could represent a reduction of up to 7 per cent, and are likely to be of particular benefit to large baseload consumers, some of whom have experienced significant price rises since privatisation.

10.61 The generators' undertakings on power station sales should increase competition significantly, thus putting downward pressure on prices in the longer term. The Director General of Electricity Supply is also consulting on a range of possible changes to the Pool which may simplify and improve trading arrangements.

10.62 The Director General is reviewing the price controls on distribution throughout Great Britain. The price controls for Northern Ireland will be reviewed before March 1997.

10.63 The Government is continuing to support the European Commission's efforts to increase competition throughout the EC as this will open up more markets to UK companies and help eliminate subsidies. The Government will also support the Commission in addressing anti-competitive practices in other EC countries which put UK industrial consumers at a disadvantage.

Gas Supply

10.64 Gas has more than a third of the industrial and commercial fuel market. It is increasingly important for power generation, accounting for 9 per cent of the market in 1993, partly because of its environmental advantages over alternatives like coal. And it is an essential feedstock for the chemical industry.

10.65 Average prices to industrial consumers in the UK are in the middle range of our competitors (chart 10.6).

10.66 Privatisation of British Gas has been followed by liberalisation and increasing competition. There are now some 35 other suppliers, who have over 75 per cent of the firm industrial market between them. Their customers are benefitting from price savings of around 10 per cent on average, with savings as high as 20 per cent in some cases.

10.67 Following the recent Report[7] from the Monopolies and Mergers Commission, the Government intends to open the tariff market to competition. A Consultation Document is being published to stimulate debate in advance of the necessary legislation.

10.68 The gas pipeline linking Northern Ireland to the mainland will be completed in 1996. Natural gas will thus become available to businesses there.

Water

10.69 Some 45 per cent of all water supplied is used in industry, agriculture and commerce. For example it takes about 30,000 litres of water to build an average car and eight pints to brew a pint of beer. It is relied upon for many industrial processes

[7]Monopolies and Mergers Commission; *Gas*. Cm 2314-2317 [HMSO] (1993)

particularly when used for cooling purposes. The supply of water in the required quantity and quality, at a competitive price, is vital to industry. And waste water has to be collected and cleaned before it can be returned to the environment.

10.70 Water and sewerage companies in England and Wales were privatised in 1989. This has provided both a major incentive to improve their efficiency and the freedom to seek business abroad. Because of the need to fund a significant investment programme, both to maintain the present infrastructure and to improve environmental standards, water charges have been rising faster than the rate of inflation during the last five years. Although there are only limited circumstances in which water companies can compete directly to supply water services to industry, the Director General of Water Services sets price limits for individual companies which provide incentives for each company to operate at the most efficient level.

10.71 Despite price increases in real terms the cost of water compares well with some other countries in Europe (notably Germany and Belgium) and the quality is excellent. In 1992 in England and Wales 98.7 per cent of over 3.75 million tests complied with the relevant water quality standards.

10.72 The water industry has in hand an investment programme of £30 billion, much of which is directed to refurbishing and improving water supply, sewerage and sewage disposal. This will benefit the UK's image abroad, help the export efforts of the water industry and underpin the attractiveness of the UK to foreign tourists thereby bolstering the important leisure and tourism industry.

New Initiatives

10.73 This chapter has set out the following new initiatives:

Communications and Broadcasting

- improved dialogue with equipment manufacturers and telecommunications operators;

- a White Paper on the future of the BBC;

- a review of media ownership restrictions;

- moves towards early introduction of digital broadcasting;

- MoD to release radio spectrum for commercial use;

- the Government will respond to the Trade and Industry Select Committee when the review of the Post Office is complete;

Transport

- delivering key improvements to the main strategic roads faster through focusing on priorities;

- the first six passenger train operating companies will be franchised in 1995, and will start to bring the benefits of private sector operation to the railways;

- progressing key transport projects under the PFI including the Second Channel Tunnel Rail Link, Heathrow Express and Crossrail;

- launch of a competition for new privately financed trains for London Underground's Northern Line;

- consultation on the privatisation of the CAA's air traffic control operations;

- consultation on developing Northolt as a business aviation facility;

- inviting local authorities to bid for funds under the new "Package Approach" to assist with the strategic development of their urban transport needs; and

Energy and Water

- consultation document on liberalising the gas market.

LONDON

11.1 London is one of the world's great cities and most important economic centres. It is a major asset for the UK economy, and vital to the competitiveness of the whole country. It:

- is one of the world's top three financial centres, and is the world's largest centre for international bank lending, contributing 75 per cent of the UK's income from financial services;

- carries out over 90 per cent of cross-border equity trading with Europe, is the global centre for raising capital on the Eurobond markets, and has about 75 per cent of international bond trading;

- contains the headquarters of the European Bank for Reconstruction and Development;

- provides a wide cultural heritage, including two of Europe's largest arts centres, two national theatre companies and over 20 museums and galleries of international standing;

- is a magnet for tourists from all over the world, contributing over 50 per cent of the UK's income from tourism;

- is a favoured location for overseas business;

- has comprehensive public transport facilities, with extensive rail, underground and bus networks, delivering improved standards of service in line with the Citizen's Charter;

- has excellent international communications, with five airports offering services to over 200 destinations worldwide, complemented very soon by the opening of the Channel Tunnel; and

- provides over 3 million jobs and offers a large pool of highly qualified and skilled people (1 in 6 of the working population of London is a graduate).

11.2 London's importance to the UK economy as a whole and the vigorous attempts by other cities in and outside Europe to acquire a greater share of mobile international business make it crucial to ensure that its prominent international position is maintained. The Government welcomes the steps already being taken by the private sector, the Corporation of London and the Bank of England to enhance London's position as a financial centre.

11.3 The new Government Office for London in close partnership with public and private sector bodies will provide concerted delivery of Government services, including:

- vigorous promotion of investment opportunities. London First, a business led group promoting London, will open a centre this year to promote inward investment in London;

- fostering substantial improvements to London's transport infrastructure, such as tendering for new privately financed trains for London Underground's Northern Line, and other initiatives described in chapter 10;

- promoting investment in London's skill-base - employment, enterprise and training - and improving education;

- developing plans for a pan-London Business Link;

- encouraging the re-use of urban land and buildings;

- initiating a wide range of measures to improve the quality of life in London; and

- publication of a London Pride prospectus, setting out a practical programme to enhance London's position over the next 15 to 20 years. London First will put together proposals for this, drawing on the work of six business-led groups investigating transport, economic development, education and training, quality of life, inward investment and tourism.

REGENERATION

12.1 The principal aims of regeneration are to improve the competitiveness of firms, the job prospects and quality of life of local people, and the social and physical environment.

12.2 The 1980s saw the laying of new foundations for urban renewal. In essence the concept was one of partnership between the public and private sectors. The early 1980s saw the establishment of Urban Development Corporations and Enterprise Zones. Urban Development Grants and City Grants, to enable projects in priority urban areas to take place, were developed. They improved upon earlier public subsidy programmes that had attracted very little private investment. Early experiments led to City Action Teams and Housing Action Trusts, which in their turn led to City Challenge, Government Regional Offices, the Single Regeneration Budget and English Partnerships. The Government's urban programme is today as sophisticated as any in the world.

CORBY

Within a year of the announcement on 1 November 1979 that production at the British Steel plant would cease, around 8,000 of the 29,000 people employed in the Corby area had been made redundant. In July 1981, unemployment reached 22.3 per cent, one of the highest rates in the UK.

The Government immediately put in place a concerted programme, building on the efforts of the Commission for the New Towns and the local authority:

- *Development Area status was granted*
- *in 1981, the Government announced that Corby was to receive the country's first Enterprise Zone*
- *in the last 14 years, over £150 million has been spent in Corby by central and local government and the Commission for the New Towns to rejuvenate local industry*

The combination of the financial support, a forward looking District Council and its geographical location have made Corby an attractive place to invest. As a result:

- *over 12,000 new jobs have been created*
- *Corby's industrial base now includes companies from a wide range of sectors, such as food processing, boat building, textiles, electronics, and printing*
- *the Enterprise Zone became the most successful in the UK*
- *every major road has been improved*
- *provision of telecommunications, electricity, gas, water, drainage and sewerage have been strengthened*

In short, Corby's economy has been transformed. In 1993, it was deemed no longer to require assisted area status. It has changed from dependence on the steel industry to one of the most diverse local economies anywhere in the country. Employment in the steel industry now accounts for 5 per cent of jobs in the Corby travel to work area, compared to 42 per cent in 1979.

12.3 Effective regeneration requires all Government policies to be applied in a coherent way, built on flexibility and partnership.

12.4 Effective partnerships have attracted substantial additional private sector resources to complement public sector spending. One example of this is the City Challenge programme introduced in 1991 to deliver the most effective regeneration schemes in England. Bids were invited from local authorities for comprehensive regeneration projects in partnership with the private sector, TECs and other public sector bodies. City Challenge areas are expected to attract some £3 billion of private sector investment alongside £1 billion of public sector money.

MANCHESTER

Stimulated by the Government's policy initiatives, the last 15 years have seen phenomenal change, with:

- *a revitalised industrial estate at Trafford Park where £170 million public investment has levered in £660 million private sector investment, attracted 615 new firms and created 10,000 jobs*
- *500 acres of dereliction and abandoned buildings cleared away in East Manchester; already the location of new sporting facilities, it is now poised for development once the last link in the motorway system is in place*
- *the new and successful commercial, housing and leisure area at Salford Quays on the site of Manchester Docks, where public investment of £30 million has led to £300 million private sector investment*
- *diversification of the economic base of the city, to include financial and commercial services and corporate headquarters, attracted by a fast growing international airport; and a city centre transformed by its new Metrolink train system and the restoration of its buildings for offices and dwellings*
- *major improvements in the living conditions of its residents, notably the £100 million City Challenge programme in Hulme to transform one of the UK's worst slums into a high quality housing and commercial area*
- *the GMEX exhibition centre, converted from a derelict railway station, and the new £40 million international concert hall, now under construction*

12.5 In the English regions, the integration of the Government Offices of four key economic departments - Environment, Employment, Trade and Industry, and Transport - and the creation of the Single Regeneration Budget have put in place powerful new regeneration mechanisms. They will have a far more proactive role in policy development for the regions and be more responsive to local priorities than has been the case. They will administer the Single Regeneration Budget, worth £1.4 billion in 1994/95, which brings together 20 existing programmes. Local partnerships will bid for resources from this budget, which will promote synergy between main programmes, with resources from Europe and the private sector. Key local players will also have the opportunity to feed in opinions and experiences to the policy making process.

12.6 Effective education and training play an important part in raising self-confidence and the quality of life in urban areas, as well as in meeting local labour market needs. The Government is working to raise standards in schools and colleges and to link them more closely to local employers. TECs, as employer-led bodies, have a vital role in working with other local partners. This work includes enhancing the level of skills and developing an integrated range of local business support services to be delivered through Business Links.

12.7 English Partnerships has been created to bring together existing regeneration measures for land reclamation and to provide industrial and commercial premises. It will operate in both urban and rural areas.

12.8 The Scottish Office's four Urban Partnership Initiatives have demonstrated the success of a broad based approach. Scottish Enterprise, Highlands and Islands Enterprise and their networks of private sector led local enterprise companies are good examples of flexible, locally-centred approaches. The lessons learned from these partnership initiatives will be applied more widely.

GLASGOW

Glasgow has emerged in the last 20 years as a pioneer in successful urban regeneration, with central Government policy and initiatives combining with strong local commitment. Progress has been evident in:

- *a transformation of the central business district brought about through partnership between public and private sectors*
- *the regeneration of inner city housing, through partnership between Scottish Homes, Glasgow District Council and the private sector*
- *a renaissance in the cultural life of the city, as exemplified in the Burrell Gallery, the new concert hall, and Glasgow's designation as European City of Culture in 1990*
- *a doubling in the number of overseas tourists visiting the city between 1982 and 1992*
- *the application of a comprehensive approach to regeneration, beginning with the Government-led GEAR project, which physically transformed the old east end of the city in a ten year programme ending in 1987*
- *the increasing use of this approach in the city's peripheral housing estates, for example the Scottish Office-led Castlemilk Partnership. This has coordinated a regeneration programme which has yielded 1,500 job placements and 500 training placements for local residents over its first five years and is well advanced in securing improvements to 3,500 houses and the building of 400 new homes*

Much remains to be done to tackle the continuing economic, social and physical problems of the city, but the experience gained over the past 20 years has given the public and private sectors and local communities the confidence to complete the regeneration task.

12.9 Partnership and flexibility have been cornerstones of regeneration efforts in Wales. The Programme for the Valleys has focused all Welsh Office responsibilities in a concerted programme to create economic opportunities in former mining areas. The Welsh Development Agency has worked closely with local authorities to provide necessary industrial infrastructure. The Cardiff Bay Development Corporation is reclaiming the former docklands in a major city development.

THE PROGRAMME FOR THE VALLEYS

The South Wales Valleys cover an area of approximately 860 square miles with 25 per cent of the population of Wales. The area contains a large proportion of disadvantaged communities.

The Government's first five year Programme for the Valleys was launched in June 1988.

The Programme involved:
- *improving over 7,000 homes*
- *creating 2.6 million square feet of industrial floorspace*
- *clearing over 2,000 acres of derelict land*
- *nearly £700 million of additional private sector investment involving 24,000 new and safeguarded jobs*
- *the successful National Garden Festival at Ebbw Vale*

A new five year Programme was launched on 1 April 1993. It aims to:
- *create more, better quality jobs*
- *improve training, education and transport so that local people can benefit*
- *improve the quality of the environment*
- *improve the health of local people*
- *improve the quality and choice of housing*

These aims will be achieved by strengthening the partnership between Government, agencies, local councils and the private and voluntary sectors under local leadership; and by increased support for local community action.

12.10 The Department of the Environment for Northern Ireland is engaged in a wide range of partnerships with local communities to revitalise many towns and villages in Northern Ireland. Two major initiatives aimed at regenerating Belfast and Londonderry have been launched and are now making good progress.

LONDONDERRY

With Government in the lead, and the City Council and the local community as active partners, the last fifteen years have seen radical transformation:
- *the infrastructure has been revitalised with a second major river crossing, the development of an ultramodern deepwater port, the opening of a regional civil airport and construction of new central railway and bus stations*
- *the housing stock has been renewed and new houses built, producing high quality private and public stock of which 70 per cent is less than 30 years old*
- *the city centre has been improved through the introduction of new shops including major retailers, new residential and office accommodation, pedestrianisation and widespread environmental improvement*
- *the 17th century city walls and associated historic core have been developed for tourism*

12.11 The Scottish, Welsh and Northern Ireland Offices and the new Government Regional Offices in England are also responsible for coordinating allocation of most of the UK's share of the European Structural Funds. This will amount to over £10 billion between 1994 and 1999. Much of this will be spent on locally developed infrastructure and training projects.

New Initiatives

12.12 The Government is taking a number of new initiatives:

- Regional Challenge, following the City Challenge model, to be introduced in England and Wales as a competition for money from the European Regional Development Fund (ERDF), the largest of the European Structural Funds. This is to encourage imaginative, value-for-money proposals, involving significant private sector funding. Subject to the European Commission's agreement to the detailed Community Support Framework documents, which govern Structural Funds money, the first competitions will be held as soon as practicable thereafter, involving total prize money of £150-200 million across the eligible English and Welsh areas. Successor competitions would follow three years later;

- the administration of the Structural Funds will be made simpler and more effective. This will be reflected in the new Community Support Frameworks;

- regional priorities and project selection criteria for the Structural Funds will be defined to favour proposals aimed at improving competitiveness; and

- the Government will consider later this year how to extend the "challenge approach" to further domestic programmes, in the light of the encouraging early experience of its effectiveness as a means of allocating public expenditure.

COMMERCIAL FRAMEWORK

REGULATION AND LAW

13.1 Businesses, their customers and their suppliers all depend on a clear and effective body of law and regulation. This basic commercial framework includes:

- planning

- environmental regulation

- standards

- competition

- commercial law

- company law

- insolvency law

- intellectual property law

13.2 The commercial framework can stimulate competition and innovation, and encourage enterprise. But if the framework is faulty it will be a constraint. It will inhibit commerce. And some businesses may simply go elsewhere.

13.3 The commercial framework must be:

- respected and trusted - so that it is used;

- lean - so it imposes no more burdens than are essential;

- clear - so that business knows what it can and cannot do;

- applied consistently - so businesses can plan ahead; and

- business oriented - so that as far as possible businesses are free to make commercial decisions without distortions caused by tax or regulation.

13.4 The readiness of companies world-wide to invest in the UK is an encouraging sign that the UK's commercial framework broadly matches business needs. But there remain areas for improvement. Crucially there is the need to ensure that regulation is applied only where it is justified, and to remove any unnecessary regulations.

Regulation

13.5 Regulation is an essential responsibility of the Government. Certain standards are rightly demanded in an advanced industrialised country. For example, consumers need protection against unsafe goods and unscrupulous dealers. The environment needs to be protected. Public health needs to be maintained. And frameworks are needed in which markets can operate. However, the Government will always consider, before regulating, whether voluntary solutions might work better.

13.6 Where regulation is necessary, its scope and implementation can affect the competitiveness of business. For example, product safety regulations protect consumers and at the same time promote market confidence and help the competitiveness of producers of quality, safe goods.

The Deregulation Initiative

13.7 The Government is pursuing four main programmes to minimise regulatory burdens on business:

- reviewing the existing regulatory system, in close consultation with business;

- bringing the Deregulation and Contracting Out Bill before Parliament;

- ensuring that future regulation is kept to the minimum and that all regulation is enforced cost-effectively; and

- developing a common approach to regulation with European partners.

13.8 The Government has just completed the first stage of a review of the 3,500 regulations affecting business. Over 500 measures have been identified for action. A process of rolling reviews of regulation will be established for the future.

HEALTH AND SAFETY REVIEW

At the Government's request, the Health and Safety Commission has carried out the most extensive review of health and safety legislation for 20 years. Some 370 sets of regulations and 28 Acts have been examined. The Commission has made wide-ranging recommendations, aimed at significantly reducing the burden on business of health and safety legislation whilst maintaining necessary health and safety standards. In its report, the Commission:

- recommends a reduction of 94 in the number of health and safety regulations in force, including the removal of over 40 per cent of those regulations which currently affect the generality of business

- sets out detailed proposals for the further simplification, clarification and modernisation of the remaining health and safety law

- proposes new and clearer guidance on specific regulations which have been criticised for their complexity; and makes recommendations aimed more generally at improving advice for business, particularly small business, on how to comply with the law

- proposes strategies which aim to make enforcement practice more coherent, consistent and effective

The Government welcomes and accepts the Commission's recommendations and will be considering with the Commission and others how best to carry them into effect. Implementation will both aid business competitiveness and, by improving the clarity of the health and safety system, result in a safer and healthier working environment.

13.9 Business has been directly involved in these reviews. Seven business task forces were set up in March 1993 and a task force for charities and voluntary associations in

August 1993. The task forces published 605 proposals on 19 January 1994. 359 have now been accepted, with 78 rejected and 168 still under consideration. For example, the Department of Health and MAFF have consulted, as the task forces recommended, on options for a simple, consistent and safe regime for food temperature controls, and are now preparing proposals.

13.10 A new Deregulation Task Force has been set up under the chairmanship of Francis Maude. It will follow up the reviews and ensure that the views of business are heard in discussions on regulation.

13.11 Changes can already be made relatively quickly to secondary legislation and to administrative procedures. But until now any amendment of regulatory provisions contained in primary legislation has had to wait until Parliamentary time was available. This has delayed much-needed reforms by years. The Deregulation and Contracting Out Bill, if approved by Parliament, will provide a mechanism for removing unnecessary burdens in existing primary legislation. The power is far-reaching. The Government has accordingly proposed stringent safeguards.

13.12 The Government is determined to ensure that further regulation does not place unnecessary burdens on business. Before new regulations can be introduced, business will be consulted and the costs and benefits fully assessed.

13.13 Enforcement can be as important as regulations themselves. Unclear guidance notes and complicated administrative arrangements can add significantly to business and other costs.

13.14 A series of reviews is in hand to remove duplication in enforcement at national and local levels, so that business does not have to deal with more inspectors than necessary. All local authority enforcement functions are being reviewed to find ways of eliminating duplication, minimising business compliance costs, promoting good practice and reducing enforcement inconsistencies through improved co-ordination.

SENSITIVE ENFORCEMENT

Ten county councils and nine other local authorities have set up local business partnerships to improve the dialogue with the business community. These partnerships help business comply with regulation by providing advice and guidance rather than by threatening prosecution.

Some 70 central Government enforcement agencies have published codes on how they can help business.

13.15 Where regulations apply internationally, under-enforcement in other countries can be as damaging to UK industry as over-enforcement in the UK. The Government will continue to press the relevant authorities to ensure that international regulations are properly enforced.

13.16 Interest in more sensitive regulation is on the increase in Europe. The Government is taking advantage of this by forming strategic alliances to place deregulation at the top of the Community agenda and to promote a burden-minimising approach to EC legislation.

Planning

13.17 The time taken for planning decisions is a major factor in influencing the location of internationally mobile projects. In the last five years the proportion of major planning applications decided within 13 weeks has increased from 57 per cent to 62 per cent.

13.18 The Government has improved the planning system by requiring all local planning authorities to prepare development plans, identifying opportunities for economic development as well as showing where environmental protection will be most important. Businesses which shape their plans in the light of local development plans should find the planning process quicker and cheaper.

13.19 But there is still room for improvement. The Government therefore proposes to consult local authorities on enabling them to agree with applicants a timetable for decision, with the applicant meeting the cost of the extra resources required.

Environmental Regulation

13.20 Environmental regulation forms an important part of the framework within which business operates. The Government will continue to seek the least prescriptive and onerous means of achieving environmental objectives. Policies will be developed on the basis of the best scientific evidence available and the best possible analysis of the balance between costs and benefits. Further steps to ease the burden on business include:

- the Government to review the procedures for alerting small businesses to new environmental regulations and for explaining them;

- Her Majesty's Inspectorate of Pollution (HMIP) to consider whether charges for Integrated Pollution Control can be discounted for companies with independently verified environmental management systems; and

- DTI and DoE to fund an evaluation of the environmental and economic effects of Integrated Pollution Control.

13.21 The world market for environmental goods and services is expected to grow to around US $320 billion by the year 2000, placing it in the same league as pharmaceuticals and aerospace. This market is strongly driven by legislation worldwide. Many UK companies have already turned environmental pressures to their advantage - the UK has a trade surplus of around £230 million in this area and is well placed to take advantage of future growth. DTI and DoE have established a Joint Environmental Markets Unit to assist companies in identifying new opportunities.

Standards

13.22 Standard measurement units and methods are essential to commerce. Increasingly, development and maintenance of measurement standards will be pursued on a European basis, with each national laboratory collaborating, or specialising, in different areas. The UK will play a full part in this.

13.23 The private sector already has an important part to play through the operation of the National Measurement Accreditation System: over 1,500 organisations, mostly in the private sector, are now accredited by DTI to make reliable tests of products and to offer calibration services traceable to national measurement standards. Through reciprocal arrangements with other countries the system also ensures that measurements and tests carried out in the UK are acceptable elsewhere - a crucial guarantee for exporters.

13.24 In the field of specification standards DTI will give greater weight to business priorities in its future support for the British Standards Institution (BSI). It has increased its support for businesspeople participating in the development of international standards. Over half of BSI's standardisation work now relates to European standards; BSI is using its influence to accelerate production of these standards. The Government will also support efforts to secure the adoption of UK standards in other countries, particularly in the developing world, on a bilateral basis.

Competition

13.25 Strong competition at home to satisfy customers also enhances the international competitiveness of our companies. The Government is committed to maintaining competition, and to introducing it wherever possible - including in industries once considered natural monopolies or the proper object of tight statutory control. For example, the abolition after 60 years of the statutory marketing arrangements for milk and potatoes will greatly enhance the competitiveness of those sectors. The competitiveness of the agricultural industry as a whole will benefit from the removal of restrictions on letting the land under the Government's proposed reform of agricultural tenancy law.

13.26 Competitive pressures will not always come from within the UK and businesses which appear to be strongly placed in the UK may still face intense competition from abroad. Mergers or joint ventures may sometimes help create companies that are large enough to take on competitors in world markets. Strategic alliances may be necessary, and indeed welcome.

13.27 Competition must not, however, be stifled nor inefficiency protected. Where necessary, cases will continue to be referred to the Monopolies and Mergers Commission. This will be done primarily on competition grounds. The competition authorities will take full account of the realities of the international business world and the Government will ensure that action following a reference is proportionate to the likely benefits.

13.28 Separate national frameworks of competition law mean that mergers involving companies in several countries could require scrutiny by a range of authorities. The EC merger regulation, administered by the European Commission, has simplified the process for large mergers which significantly affect trade within the EC.

13.29 Overall the Government believes that UK competition law strikes as good a balance as that of other countries between effective regulation and the avoidance of excessive burdens on business. It recognises, however, that the existing legislation on restrictive trade practices is a relative weakness. The Government is committed to introducing legislation to reform the law on restrictive trade practices and abuse of market power as soon as Parliamentary time permits.

13.30 The Deregulation and Contracting Out Bill will make the existing UK law less burdensome. It will extend the scope for companies to offer undertakings as an alternative to a detailed investigation by the Monopolies and Mergers Commission. In addition, insignificant cases are being removed from scrutiny. Target times for decisions will be shortened.

13.31 The Government is also encouraging the European Commission to reduce delays in its handling of cases under Articles 85 and 86 of the Treaty of Rome, to continue to demonstrate that businesses are treated fairly, and to ensure transparency and consistency in its policy on fines.

Commercial law

13.32 The law must provide rights, obligations and remedies which promote sound commercial practice. It should facilitate the establishment of solid commercial relationships, and provide remedies which are in tune with commercial needs if a dispute arises.

13.33 The strengths of the UK commercial system include a recognised and well established framework of commercial law, and the expertise and reputation of the legal profession. Three-quarters of all cases taken in the Commercial Court involve at least one foreign party, and invisible earnings from the provision of legal services amount to some £500 million a year.

13.34 Despite these strengths, litigation can be an expensive and time-consuming way of obtaining redress. In some cases businesses may prefer a relatively quick and cheap settlement. Arbitration is confidential and can, if agreed, be legally binding. It may also be cheaper and quicker than litigation. The Government has recently published a consultation paper[1] on consolidation and simplification of arbitration law in England and Wales and proposals for the development and reform of arbitration in Scotland are currently under preparation by a Committee reporting to the Lord Advocate.

13.35 The Government is also keen to encourage the use in appropriate cases of other forms of alternative dispute resolution. This is of particular use to SMEs as disputes can often be resolved in one day. The Centre for Dispute Resolution is making an increasingly important contribution and schemes for alternative dispute resolution have recently been established by the Faculty of Advocates and the Law Society of Scotland.

13.36 The Law Commissions in England and Wales and in Scotland play a fundamental role in reviewing legislation to ensure the law is as clear as possible in a complex world. They would welcome contact from any sector of the business community which feels that there are problems with the way in which business law operates. The Law Commission for England and Wales is undertaking a study of the role of trust law in the commercial field, where it is important for example as a means of combating fraud and recovering misappropriated property.

Company law

13.37 Company law must continue to adapt to modern conditions. Areas currently under review, with the help of business interests, include:

- making it easier for companies to be run as groups without undermining the legitimate interests of creditors;

- simplifying company law for small, owner-managed companies; and

- clarifying directors' duties.

Consultation documents are being issued as proposals are developed. Present plans are to issue papers on group law and on directors' duties this autumn.

[1]*A consultative paper on draft clauses and schedules of an Arbitration Bill.* [DTI] (1994)

> **ACTION TO HELP SMALL COMPANIES**
> *The solutions that are suitable for large companies may not be suitable for smaller ones:*
> - *when regulations are made in the summer up to half a million small companies will be allowed to dispense with the statutory audit requirement*
> - *small companies can already present less information in their statutory accounts than large ones. The Government has supported the adoption of EC proposals to classify more companies as small and it will consult widely on implementation*
> - *at the request of the Accounting Standards Board, the Consultative Committee of Accountancy Bodies is looking at the application of accounting standards to small companies and hopes to consult on proposals in the summer*
> - *the Government has commissioned a feasibility study by the Law Commission on the best way forward for reform of the law for small private companies*

13.38 The private sector is also playing a key role. The Financial Reporting Council, its subsidiaries, and the Auditing Practices Board are improving standards of financial reporting. The accountancy profession is heavily engaged in this work. The Government welcomes the debate on moves to improve effectiveness by bringing together the professional associations. The Government also welcomes the moves under the Financial Reporting Council to co-ordinate the timing of proposals for reform of financial reporting, and will keep the Council informed over the timing of its own consultation on company law.

Insolvency law

13.39 Insolvency law aims to provide a fair system of economic rehabilitation for both companies and individuals. The Government welcomes cases where receivers work with managers to achieve a beneficial solution. Unviable businesses should be wound up in an orderly fashion, but there should be a range of effective rescue mechanisms for viable companies with temporary business problems.

13.40 A recent practice note by the Vice Chancellor should make entry into administration quicker and cheaper. The last Budget included tax changes which made company voluntary arrangements more attractive. Discussion on issues arising from the recent DTI consultation on company rescues will continue over the next few months.

13.41 But, as well as changes to law and practice, creditors will need to have a constructive attitude and companies will have to recognise at an early stage that they are heading for trouble. Responsibility for this lies with their directors, their lenders and their professional advisers.

13.42 The recent judgment of the Court of Appeal in Paramount Airways has highlighted factors which would have made it more difficult for viable companies to be rescued. The Government moved quickly to enable administrative receivers and administrators to keep on employees without adopting all the liabilities the Paramount judgment implied.

Intellectual property law

13.43 Companies need an efficient system of registration and protection of patents, trade marks, registered designs and copyrights.

13.44 The cost of obtaining protection for intellectual property in the UK is low compared to our major competitors. But the cost of defending it against encroachment can be high. Patent litigation here is much more expensive than in France or Germany, though not nearly as expensive as in the US. The Government has established Patent County Courts, which provide a quicker and potentially cheaper way of resolving disputes in this field. But costs will only be reduced if companies choose to use less expensive representation than in the High Court.

13.45 The Government has introduced a Trade Marks Bill to streamline and simplify the domestic registration of trade marks and to ratify the Protocol to the Madrid Agreement on Trade Marks. Companies will be able to gain trade mark protection in up to thirty countries on the basis of a single filing in the UK. This will further simplify procedures and reduce costs. The Government has acted to permit patent agents and registered trade mark agents to work together in large mixed partnerships.

New Initiatives

13.46 The main new initiatives are:

- continued progress on deregulation: 359 business task force recommendations now accepted; HSC recommendations to reduce and simplify health safety regulations - while preserving standards - to be taken forward; new Deregulation Task Force established;

- consultation on arrangements to allow applicants for planning permission to agree a timetable for decisions with local authorities and meet the cost of extra resources;

- HMIP to consider whether charges for Integrated Pollution Control can be discounted for companies with independently verified environmental management systems;

- consultation on new, simplified, arbitration law;

- consultation on increasing size limit for small companies to take advantage of accounting disclosure concessions; and

- forthcoming consultation documents on changes to company law.

TAXATION

13.47 A country's tax regime affects its competitiveness. While the prime purpose of taxation is to raise revenue to fund essential public services, a burdensome regime can stifle growth.

13.48 Tax policy is inevitably a compromise between conflicting demands. The Government aims to:

- keep the overall tax burden as low as possible, through firm control over public spending;

- reduce marginal tax rates on income and profits, to sharpen incentives to work and create wealth;

- maintain a broad tax base which helps to keep tax rates low and avoids distorting commercial decisions;

- shift the balance of taxation from taxes on income to taxes on spending;

- simplify the administration of the tax system and minimise the burdens which compliance places on the taxpayer;

- ensure that the tax system is applied fairly and evenly, closing loopholes so that commercial decisions are not distorted by attempts to avoid tax;

- use the tax system to make markets work better, for example by making decision makers aware of the external costs of their decisions; and

- ensure that revenue is raised in ways which do least harm to economic efficiency and take account of the competitive position of UK industry.

Keeping the tax burden low

13.49 The overall tax burden in the UK is a good deal lower than in many of our competitors. In 1991, the latest year for which full international comparisons are available, total tax revenue as a percentage of GDP in the UK was 36 per cent. This was lower than all other EC countries except Spain and Portugal. Even after the tax increases announced in last year's Budgets, tax revenues, as a percentage of GDP, will still be below the 1991 EC average of 41 per cent.

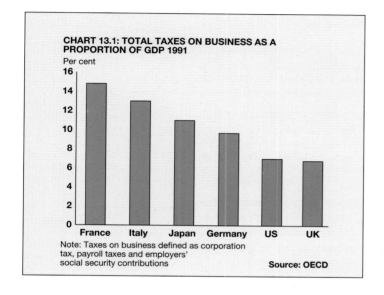

CHART 13.1: TOTAL TAXES ON BUSINESS AS A PROPORTION OF GDP 1991

Per cent

Note: Taxes on business defined as corporation tax, payroll taxes and employers' social security contributions

Source: OECD

13.50 International comparisons of the tax burden on businesses are difficult to make. Taking the three main taxes on business - taxes on corporate profits, employers' social security costs and payroll taxes - together, the UK compares favourably (chart 13.1). On this measure, business taxes amount to 7 per cent of GDP in the UK compared to 10 per cent in Germany, 11 per cent in Japan and 15 per cent in France.

Reducing taxes on enterprise

13.51 The main rate of corporation tax has been reduced since 1979 from 52 per cent to 33 per cent and is now the lowest of any major industrial country. Although care is needed when making international comparisons (since corporate tax structures and the treatment of capital spending and dividends differ considerably between countries) rates of profits taxes, including local taxes, are around 40 per cent in the US, 50 per cent in Japan and 56 per cent (on undistributed profits) in Germany.

13.52 The present corporation tax structure reflects the Government's preference for taxing at a low rate on a broad base to avoid distortion to commercial decisions. While there are continuing calls for a return to higher levels of capital allowances, the present rate of 25 per cent is close to normal commercial rates of depreciation. For certain types of asset with a shorter economic life, a more generous scheme applies.

13.53 The UK has an especially favourable tax regime for small companies. About five out of six companies which pay corporation tax, do so at the small companies' rate. This tax rate has been reduced since 1979 from 42 per cent to 25 per cent. Since 1988 the threshold below which companies pay tax at this lower rate has been trebled.

13.54 The Government has recently introduced changes which will help UK companies expand and compete in international markets. From July 1994 the foreign income dividend scheme will allow companies to pay less UK tax when they distribute profits earned from abroad. The reduction in the rate of Advance Corporation Tax (ACT) from 25 per cent to 20 per cent will have a similar effect on companies with surplus ACT.

13.55 Capital taxation has been reformed to encourage entrepreneurs:

- most actively trading businesses are effectively exempt from inheritance tax;

- the overwhelming majority of proprietors selling their businesses on retirement pay no tax on their gains; and

- the 1994 Finance Act includes a new relief enabling individuals to defer tax on capital gains if they reinvest in an unquoted trading company.

13.56 The Government has also:

- abolished several taxes on business, including the national insurance surcharge and development land tax;

- opposed EC proposals for a carbon energy tax on the grounds that it would increase business costs and hurt competitiveness; and

- limited the rise in business rate poundage to the rate of inflation.

Sharpening incentives

13.57 Income tax rates have been reduced sharply, allowing individuals and the owners of unincorporated businesses to keep more of their earnings. Since 1979:

- the basic rate of tax has been cut from 33 per cent to 25 per cent, and a lower rate of 20 per cent has been introduced for the first £3,000 of taxable income;

- the top rate of income tax on earned income has been reduced from 83 per cent to 40 per cent;

- the top rate on investment income (which includes dividends) has fallen from 98 per cent to 40 per cent. The combined top rate of tax and social security contributions is now 40 per cent. This is the lowest in the EC, matched only by Greece; and

- the number of tax rates has been reduced from 11 to three.

Keeping down employment costs

13.58 The structure of employers' National Insurance Contributions (NICs) has been made more progressive in order to reduce employment costs. Employers pay significantly reduced rates for employees with weekly earnings below £200. From April 1994, these rates were cut by 1 per cent. Employers with workers earning over £200 a week saw a reduction in their NICs of 0.2 per cent. These reductions more than make up for the loss of reimbursement of Statutory Sick Pay from the same date and the additional costs of Statutory Maternity Pay from September this year.

Simplifying administration

13.59 A wide range of initiatives have cut compliance costs for businesses and simplified the administration regime. These include:

- increases in the VAT threshold to £45,000. This is five times higher than the EC average. The VAT penalty regime has also been eased and simplified;

- introduction of a pay and file system for corporation tax in 1993. This has streamlined payment of tax and allows companies to assess their own bills;

- simplification of personal tax. In the next three years the rules for taxing the self employed will be reformed. Self assessment will be introduced for all those who submit tax returns; and

- plans to consult business on the closer alignment of definitions used in assessing NICs and income tax to simplify work for employers.

New Initiatives

13.60 The Treasury is currently engaged in a broad dialogue with industry about the treatment of savings and the flow of funds to business. This work is discussed in the Finance for Business chapter. It:

- is looking at the impact of the tax system on the costs and returns to different providers and users of finance and on different forms of finance; and

- will inform policy over the period ahead.

13.61 In addition the Government is looking at how the work of the Inland Revenue, Customs and Excise and the Contributions Agency can best be coordinated to minimise costs on business arising from tax collection and compliance.

BUSINESS OF GOVERNMENT

14.1 Competitiveness is not just an issue for the private sector. The public sector must be efficient and effective to work in partnership with industry. If it is not well-managed, it can impose unnecessary burdens on UK companies through: taxes that could have been more productively spent, or lifted altogether; poorly provided services; and delayed responses while business opportunities slip away.

14.2 In common with other developed countries, the UK needs high quality public services. These have to be funded, for the most part, by the taxpayer. The Government has sought to minimise that burden on the taxpayer by a fundamental reversal of the long-term growth of the public sector. In 1979, at its peak, the public sector employed nearly 7½ million people. By 1993, that figure had fallen by about a fifth to under 6 million. This reduction is continuing.

14.3 The output of many key public services is vital to the economic success and competitiveness of the UK as a nation. Many of these services - like education and training or help for exporters - are discussed elsewhere in this White Paper. All these services must be effectively managed, responsive to customer requirements, and focused on high quality outputs.

The Government's approach - a public service reform programme

14.4 This programme promotes efficiency and effectiveness in the public sector. Many of its elements have been in place since 1979. The Citizen's Charter, introduced in 1991, is central to the reforms, and is intended to be a ten-year programme of improvement, stretching into the next century. The reform programme will create a new partnership of ideas and experience between private and public sectors.

Making services more efficient

14.5 Since 1979, the Government has progressively concentrated on providing only those functions which are both necessary and best carried out in the public sector. This cutting back has not been restricted to trading activities, but has spanned the whole public service. It has involved:

- **direct abolition wherever feasible**. For example, the general streamlining of employment practices has seen the abolition of the Dock Labour Scheme and the Wages Councils. A substantial range of public functions carried out by Non Departmental Public Bodies ("quangos") has been abolished, and there are currently almost 800 fewer of these bodies than in 1979;

- **privatisation** where an activity no longer needs to be carried out in the public sector. By the end of the last financial year (1993/94), 47 major activities and many smaller ones had been privatised. And the programme continues, both in the nationalised industries - British Rail, British Coal - and in the rest of the public sector. Forthcoming privatisations include subsidiary companies of London Bus Ltd; the Royal Dockyards; the Crown Agents; the National Engineering Laboratory; the Laboratory of the Government Chemist and the Transport Research Laboratory; and

---

REVIEW OF GOVERNMENT RESEARCH LABORATORIES

An efficiency scrutiny is examining the government reseach establishments sector by sector. It will identify those where privatisation is feasible and desirable, and will make recommendations on the potential for rationalisation in other cases.

- **contracting-out**, where the Government retains ultimate responsibility for a service, but enables the private sector to compete for a contract to run it. In some cases (for example, new functions required by statute), the service will often be contracted-out from the outset. In others there will be a competition (a "market test") between in-service and external providers to see whether the public or private sector can undertake the work more cost-effectively.

14.6 In this way, huge areas of government activity have been opened up to competitive provision. In 1992/93, local government and the NHS alone put out to competitive tender activities with a value of more than £7 billion, of which about £2.6 billion was won by the private sector. The range of functions subject to competitive contract is continuing to expand into new areas such as support services for the police.

COMPETING FOR QUALITY PROGRAMME

Under the "Competing for Quality" programme Government departments examined activities worth £1.1 billion over the period April 1992-December 1993. These activities were either abolished, privatised, contracted out or market tested. Departments are committed to a further programme of £830 million in the period to September 1994, and have submitted outline plans for the following three years.

> ### *LOCAL AUTHORITIES: COMPULSORY COMPETITIVE TENDERING*
> - *The introduction of Compulsory Competitive Tendering (CCT) in 1980 has raised the quality of services and reduced local authority costs to the taxpayer and to industry*
> - *Around £6 billion of services a year are now subject to CCT. Tendering is currently being extended to local authority professional services in areas such as IT, finance, engineering and property, worth a further £6 billion a year*
> - *CCT has created a thriving private sector where none previously existed, for example street cleaning, refuse collection, and the maintenance of public parks and gardens*

14.7 For those activities which remain within government, there are continuous efficiency programmes, carried out through both specific reviews and tight running cost controls. In central government, savings from efficiency reviews since 1979 have amounted to more than £2 billion. In the NHS, efficiency in the hospital and community health services has increased by over 20 per cent since 1979, and a target of a further 2¼ per cent increase has been set for 1994/95.

Making services more effective

14.8 In the past, questions about the effectiveness of public services concentrated on inputs, not outputs. What was spent was often seen as more important, and was certainly easier to measure, than the quality of what was achieved. There was insufficient focus on the quality of service to the user or customer.

14.9 Those attitudes had to change. Companies whose survival was challenged in the 1980s had no choice but to improve performance dramatically. In the public sector, this process was not automatic. Yet it is being achieved nonetheless, through the Citizen's Charter, and the re-structuring of key public services.

The Citizen's Charter

14.10 The Citizen's Charter has brought a new, long-term emphasis on responsiveness to the customer. All main public services are already covered by 39 individual Charters and other related initiatives designed to improve performance, openness and responsiveness, as well as setting out the standards of service the customer has a right to expect. Some examples are shown below - many others can be found in the recent "Citizen's Charter Second Report" White Paper[1].

---

[1] *Citizen's Charter Second Report*. Cm 2540 [HMSO] (1994)

THE CITIZEN'S CHARTER: EXAMPLES

- *Education - publication of wide-ranging comparative league tables of schools' performance*
- *NHS - publication of comparative information on hospital and ambulance service performance from June 1994*
- *British Rail - progressive raising of punctuality and reliability targets*
- *Local Authorities - publication of comparative data on performance against targets for dealing with a large number of services*
- *Post Office - 1992/93 "next working day" first class letter delivery target of 90.5 per cent achieved; target raised to 92 per cent for 1993/94*
- *Customs and Excise - commitment to release at least 90 per cent of consignments within 4 working hours (electronic declaration) or 12 working hours (paper declaration). 95 per cent of VAT registration processed within three weeks of receipt*
- *Companies House (development of computerised annual returns and remote user systems) and Patent Office (late hours fax services and other customer care initiatives) awarded Charter Mark for excellence in service delivery*
- *National Museums and Galleries - to draw up performance standards under the Citizen's Charter*

Restructuring of key services throughout the public sector

14.11 The setting and achievement of specific performance targets, standards of service and other Charter commitments is critically dependent on organisational structures which can respond quickly and clearly to the needs of customers. A series of major initiatives since the mid 1980s is enabling public service providers to be more clearly responsible for the quality of service they offer and more responsive to the requirements placed on them:

- since 1988 executive functions of central government have increasingly been carried out by separate **executive agencies**, with substantial delegated management control. Many of these agencies, like the Employment Service, Companies House and Patent Office, have a vital role in supporting UK competitiveness. Each agency has a chief executive who is responsible for the agency's performance. Ministers set key targets for agencies, and look for continued improvement in quality year-by-year. Each agency is reviewed periodically under the Government's "prior options" programme to see whether its functions can be abolished, privatised, contracted-out or market tested;

EXECUTIVE AGENCIES: PROGRESS

- *Progress on Agencies in Central Government was recently set out in the White Paper "Next Steps Review 1993"[2]*
- *Since that Review, a further six Agencies have been launched*
- *78 per cent of the Civil Service works in Agencies or announced candidates for Agency status*

---

[2]*Next Steps – Agencies in Government Review 1993.* Cm 2430 [HMSO] (1993)

- the **NHS reforms** are now firmly in place, shifting power towards the patient and giving local health authorities, NHS Trusts and GP fund holders the freedom to innovate and improve patient services;

- **grant maintained** status gives schools the right to manage their own affairs. This allows teachers, parents and governors to choose what kind of school they want, producing diversity and providing parents with more choice for their children;

- several ambitious intiatives have been undertaken to improve the responsiveness and accessibility of **Government services** at the local level. TECs (lecs in Scotland) develop local strategies to boost the skill levels of the UK labour force. A network of one-stop shops, called Business Links, is being set up in England to offer a full, high quality range of services to business. One-stop shops are also being created in Scotland, and improvement of business services delivery is being considered in Wales;

- the regional work of four key economic departments – Environment, Employment, Trade and Industry and Transport – has been brought together into a **single Government Office** for each English Region making Government more responsive to local priorities and need. This enables Government to tackle policy development and implementation in a more cohesive way, and helps focus the Government's support for competitiveness;

- subject to the necessary legislation, the creation of a smaller number of **unitary authorities** from existing councils in many areas will remove a tier of bureaucracy, end conflict in the present two-tier planning system and offer greater scope for the amalgamation of services for the private sector to win contracts; and

- reforms to the **police service** in the Police and Magistrates Courts Bill seek to give police authorities and chief constables greater freedom and responsibility for delivering a policing service which meets local needs, including those of business.

Public and Private Sectors - a partnership of ideas and expertise

14.12 The Government is forging a partnership between the public and private sectors based on shared experience and expertise in management techniques. Ideas are developing on a common basis in a number of areas:

- **pay** is by far the largest single element (over 50 per cent) of total running costs in the Civil Service. Excessive settlements or those not matched by service improvements can add enormously to costs and distort labour markets. The Government is determined that the public sector approach to pay should reflect experience in the private sector, particularly the emphasis on funding pay increases through improvements in productivity. In 1994/95 any pay increases for public sector employees are to be offset by improvements in productivity. Within these overall constraints, substantial delegations of pay bargaining processes are being implemented. For example, Inland Revenue, Customs and Excise and the Health and Safety Executive together with 21 of the largest agencies already have responsibility for pay negotiations. This will be extended in 1995;

- **performance-related pay** schemes are being implemented across the public sector. Details of these schemes can be found in the Citizen's Charter Second Report;

- **accruals accounting** has already been introduced in key areas of the public sector which provide services such as the NHS and executive agencies. Plans are being developed for its introduction in the rest of central government, providing, for the first time, a proper measure of the costs of resources which government consumes each year;

- delegation of management responsibility and control within the public sector has required the introduction of techniques widely used in business **to improve performance**. Examples are priority-based management information systems and budgets; Total Quality Management Systems; BS5750, and benchmarking; and

- **interchange** between the Civil Service and industry and commerce has long been encouraged. Recent developments have accelerated that process. The numbers involved in interchange with the private sector have almost trebled since 1979. In 1993 there were over 600 secondments as well as a variety of short-term attachments (including more than 60 at senior levels as part of a planned, Service-wide programme). About 60 civil servants currently serve as non-executive directors, the majority in private sector companies. A new initiative has been launched to increase these opportunities. Government departments and agencies are more open than ever before to outside skills and expertise. In 1993, nearly a quarter of vacancies in the top three grades was filled by open competition. It has been normal practice to recruit agency chief executives in this way, and 38 of these posts - over 40 per cent of the total - are currently held by people who are not career civil servants. A recent survey showed that over half the top 650 civil servants already possess outside experience, including experience gained in industry or business.

> ### *CONTINUING AGENDA FOR CIVIL SERVICE REFORM*
> * *The systematic review of central government is leading to a new structure, with smaller centres of departments and their executive functions organised in agencies or provided by the private sector. Work is in hand on a range of changes designed to improve performance both in the centres of departments and in agencies*
> * *As part of this, the Government is considering the future development of the senior Civil Service following the Efficiency Unit review of Career Management and Succession Planning for the senior Civil Service*
> * *Between April 1979 and October 1993, the number of civil servants fell by 25 per cent from over 730,000 to fewer than 550,000. This number will continue to fall*

Britain - a world leader in Public Service Reform

14.13 Throughout the developed world, governments are faced with common pressures to ensure that public services are delivered efficiently and effectively and in ways which are responsive to the needs of the citizen. Elements in the Government's own reform programme (privatisation, deregulation, cutting red tape and so on) can be found in a number of countries. But the long term, comprehensive, nature of the public service programme here places the UK amongst the world leaders in this field. Indeed, it has been said that 'Statecraft is becoming a major British export, just as privatisation was in the 1980s'[3].

> ### *PUBLIC SERVICE REFORM : INTERNATIONAL EXAMPLES*
> *New Zealand: legislation passed between 1988-91 has resulted in:*
> * *devolvement of most government functions to crown agencies and state businesses*
> * *five-year renewable contracts for heads of departments and some other senior civil servants*
> * *annual performance agreements between Ministers and Chief Executives*
> * *accruals accounting in government*
>
> *USA: Vice-President Gore's "National Performance Review" launched in September 1993, includes radical State and local government programmes. These increase efficiency, contract-out functions, and improve customer services. Review targets include:*
> * *12 per cent reduction in civilian public service workforce by 1998*
> * *all Federal Agency internal regulations to be reviewed within three years, with a goal of 50 per cent reduction*
> * *elimination of monopolies in many Federal Government Support Services*
> * *development of written performance agreements between the President and Department and Agency heads*

New initiatives

14.14 To maintain the momentum of its radical programme of public sector reform, the Government will:

* publish a White Paper on the Civil Service setting out its conclusions on the Efficiency Unit's review of Career Management and Succession Planning for the Senior Civil Service[4];

[3]The Times; *Editorial.* (26 October 1993)

[4]*Career Management and Succession Planning Study.* [HMSO] (1993)

- evaluate the Competing for Quality initiative to see how best it can be developed in future years, including by making greater use of innovative ideas and approaches from the private sector;

- announce the timing and terms of all reviews of proposed or existing agencies, as well as large executive NDPBs. This will enable outside organisations to put forward innovative ideas on how their functions might most effectively be carried out; and

- ask the Efficiency Unit to review management planning and control systems in departments. The aim is to ensure that these systems reflect the new structure of central government and best practice developed in the public and private sectors over the last decade.

Public Purchasing

15.1 The public sector is by far the largest purchaser of goods and services in the UK. In 1993 central and local Government spent some £74 billion purchasing goods and services, some 15 per cent of GDP. Further opportunities for suppliers are being generated by the Government's market testing programme, opening new areas to competition.

15.2 So the importance of the public sector as a purchaser is fundamental. Many sectors of UK industry (such as defence equipment and construction) are heavily dependent on its decisions. Good purchasing can have a profound effect on the competitiveness of firms. It can improve quality, assist innovation, reduce costs, set standards, and provide a shop window for world sales.

15.3 In exercising its purchasing power, the Government has two fundamental aims:

- value for money; and

- improving the competitiveness of its suppliers.

15.4 These aims are complementary. To win public contracts in competition, suppliers need to produce good quality, keenly priced goods and services. This is of mutual benefit to public sector customers, and the taxpayer, and to suppliers themselves who will be in a better position to win business internationally. Seeking value for money through competition contributes to a sound industrial and commercial base.

15.5 Equally helping suppliers through a constructive partnership, rather than a short-term arm's length, adversarial relationship, will lead to cost savings as well as improving quality and service delivery to the mutual benefit of both customer and supplier. Such a partnership needs to be established by competitive tender and reopened periodically to competition.

15.6 Internationally, the Government aims to secure agreements under which UK suppliers can gain access to public sector markets abroad and to ensure the effective implementation of these agreements.

Progress to date

15.7 The public sector is highly diverse. It includes central Government departments and agencies, the National Health Service and local authorities. The EC public procurement directives extend to private sector utilities. Individual departments and agencies are responsible for the effectiveness and efficiency of their procurement. Public procurement therefore is not a monolith, but the aggregate of a multitude of individual decisions.

15.8 Against this background, the Government has since 1981 promoted the spread of best practice through its guidelines on public procurement. Its policy is:

- to give early warning to its suppliers of potential requirements, but without distorting competition. This applies particularly to new or improved technology. For instance the MoD's Pathfinder Programme, launched in 1992, offers business an opportunity for early involvement in defence research, and the chance to align its own research with that of MoD;

- to encourage product and process improvement and innovation. For example, the Department of Environment is working closely with leading building specifiers, contractors and product suppliers to establish appropriate benchmarks and to improve the competitive performance of suppliers;

- to specify requirements in output performance terms and frame specifications around appropriate standards to achieve economies of scale and help exports;

- to encourage quality certification and quality assurance (requiring BS5750 or equivalent where appropriate);

- to encourage, where cost-effective, aggregation of demand; the Home Office has for instance negotiated a number of national supply arrangements on behalf of individual police authorities, for example for vehicles and IT services; and

- to debrief suppliers on request, including identifying specific deficiencies in bids.

15.9 But policy guidance is not enough by itself. It needs to be implemented on the ground. The Central Unit on Procurement (CUP), set up in the Treasury in 1986, has taken a number of initiatives to improve the professionalism and operational effectiveness of Government procurement:

- experts have been recruited from the private sector to introduce and develop **professionalism** amongst Government staff. There is regular exchange of ideas with the professional institutions and the private sector, and the Government is encouraging university research into procurement topics;

- the Government is committed to improve the level of **training** of those engaged in Government procurement at all levels. A new two year professional training programme was introduced in 1990. Some 45 per cent of staff in key posts have completed or are involved in this;

- **management information systems** are being introduced to improve information and control. For example the Purchasing and Supply Unified

Information Technology (PURSUIT) specifications developed by CUP will help automate routine tasks and incorporate best practice. 11 PURSUIT-based systems have been installed and 58 more are planned over the next four years. Departments are also developing paperless standardised Electronic Data Interchange (EDI). Twenty departments are planning to introduce such systems. Both systems will help suppliers in dealing with Government purchasers through greater efficiency and time savings;

- the Government is committed to explaining and improving procurement through **guidance** notes issued by CUP. These are also available to suppliers to help them understand Government procedures. For small firms in particular, DTI has issued advice on how to sell to Government; and

- **environmental strategies** are reflected in Government specifications for goods and services. DoE, for example, has recently published guidance to its suppliers on improving quality while reducing the impact on the environment.

Success to date

15.10 Significant value for money improvements have been achieved. Figures collected from the main spending departments show that value for money savings of about 5 per cent have been achieved for each of the past five years, worth some £1.3 billion. Further information is in the CUP's annual report to the Prime Minister[1].

15.11 International comparisons are difficult to make. But the Government is committed to the exchange of ideas and experience with overseas Governments. It is also committed to monitoring best private sector practice with a view to applying it in the public sector.

European Community

15.12 Legislation to open up public contracts to competition has been successfully achieved. The rules apply to supplies, works, a wide range of services as well as the utilities in the water, energy, transport and telecommunications sectors. For the first time, Member States must make legal remedies available so that suppliers and contractors can enforce their rights. Since 1 January 1994 the rights and obligations under the EC procurement directives have been extended to Austria, Finland, Iceland, Norway and Sweden on a reciprocal basis.

15.13 While welcome, the new Single Market legislation is not a guarantee of open markets. The Government will be monitoring its impact closely to ensure that in

[1] *Government Purchasing: Report to the Prime Minister 1992* [HMSO] (1993)

practice it does increase the opportunities for competitive suppliers without placing unnecessary burdens on suppliers or purchasers. The Government will continue to encourage the Commission to improve its monitoring of the public procurement rules, the transparency of these rules, and its effectiveness in handling complaints.

GATT Government Procurement Agreement

15.14 The proposed new GATT Agreement on Government Procurement will come into effect on 1 January 1996, following closely the existing EC rules. This extension will lead to a ten-fold increase in the value of public purchases subject to the Agreement. It will provide new opportunities for competitive UK suppliers and contractors. It guarantees access in particular sectors to countries which have made similar guarantees. These are likely to include Canada, Israel, Japan, Korea, Switzerland and the US.

New Initiatives

15.15 A number of initiatives are planned:

- the Treasury, in collaboration with other departments, will develop by January 1995 a strategy to improve **value for money** and the **competitiveness of suppliers.** Key elements will be:

  - a published standard designed to achieve professionalism and best value for money in procurement;

  - a particular focus on the management of large service contracts and, with the Department of the Environment, on developing good practice in construction procurement, designed to combine best value for money with the encouragement of a strong and competitive industry; and

  - encouragement to all departments and agencies to develop further and better performance indicators for procurement.

- the Government believes that its purchasing practices should be tested against world-class standards. In collaboration with the professional institutions and universities, it will further develop effective **benchmarking** systems. It will seek views from suppliers and other interested parties on existing performance, and provide for appropriate independent comparisons with best private sector practice. Progress will be reported in CUP's annual progress report to the Prime Minister on 1994;

- a new target will be set that, by end 1996, 75 per cent of staff in key procurement posts in central Government should either have professional qualifications, or have completed its two year professional **training** programme;

- like any large company in the private sector the Government recognises the benefits of encouraging its suppliers. It will therefore encourage the spread of best practice in **supplier development** in the public sector, working, as appropriate, with Partnership Sourcing Ltd and professional bodies. It will also seek to provide market information to new suppliers. In this context, the proposed regional supply networks will work with major purchasers, including those in the public sector, to promote the capabilities of the regional supply base;

- the Government will continue to look at making it easier and simpler for companies of all sizes to bid for public contracts. Particular attention will be paid to **avoidance of over-specification and unnecessary red tape**. Progress will be reported in CUP's annual progress report to the Prime Minister on 1994;

- the Government will review by end 1994 the help currently provided to **SMEs** in bidding for public (and private) sector contracts to see whether more can be done to encourage SME participation. The review will take account of measures adopted in overseas countries; and

- the Government will closely monitor the impact of the new legislation in the **EC** to ensure that in practice it increases opportunities for competitive suppliers. It will take advantage of reviews of the legislation to work to reduce bureaucracy and encourage the development of best practice.

NEXT STEPS

16.1 Competitiveness is an increasingly prominent feature on the agenda in many countries. The Trade and Industry Select Committee has recently published a Report setting out its analysis of UK manufacturing competitiveness; the Government is replying separately to its recommendations. This White Paper sets out the Government's view of the UK's competitive position. It provides, in a time span outside the normal cut and thrust of party politics, an assessment of the UK's relative strengths and weaknesses – those factors which fundamentally determine a nation's international standing.

16.2 Whether reporting on areas where the UK is ahead, or where it still needs to catch up, on one conclusion there can be no doubt. The UK – as other nations – is under relentless pressure. The international competition for jobs, markets and talented people is fierce and getting fiercer.

16.3 This White Paper reports on matters already announced and in progress. It also reports on a number of initiatives on which the Government has been working and which it is timely to announce in this context. In addition, a number of initiatives is reported where the conclusions will only be reached later in the year.

16.4 This White Paper is, in effect, a snapshot of the work in hand across Government. It shows a formidable agenda of action and initiatives. It reveals the comprehensive nature of the Government's work and how it can support wealth creation.

16.5 At the head of this approach is a recognition that the UK needs a culture of continuing improvement. Competitiveness is dynamic. We cannot ever afford to stand still. For as we change and innovate, the outside world also changes. And so the pressures continue.

16.6 For these reasons, the approach to the nation's competitiveness must be one of continual review. The Ministerial Group on Competitiveness will remain in existence and this White Paper, in whole or part, will be updated, as appropriate, from time to time.

16.7 This White Paper sets out how the Government is planning to support UK industry. But it will take a continuing effort from *all* of us to ensure the UK remains competitive.

GLOSSARY

Assisted Areas
Areas eligible for Regional Industrial Assistance under the Industrial Development Act 1982

BSI
British Standards Institution

Business Links
See boxes on pages 67 and 70

CAA
Civil Aviation Authority

Cadbury Committee
A committee chaired by Sir Adrian Cadbury that recommended changes to corporate governance in the UK

CAP
Common Agricultural Policy

CBI
Confederation of British Industry

CDLs
Career Development Loans - private sector loans to individuals (with government-funded interest holiday) to fund training

Compacts
Agreements between employers, schools and young people where young people work towards personal targets in return for employer-related incentives

CSO
Central Statistical Office

CUP
H M Treasury's Central Unit on Procurement

Deregulation
See paras 13.7 – 13.16

DFE
Department for Education

DoE
Department of the Environment

DTI
Department of Trade and Industry

DTp
Department of Transport

EC
European Community, composed of Belgium, Denmark, Germany, Greece, Spain, France, the Republic of Ireland, Italy, Luxembourg, the Netherlands, Portugal and the United Kingdom (in the charts, unless otherwise stated, figures for the EC include figures for the UK)

EC Framework Programme
R&D programmes covering a wide range of generic technologies

ECGD
Export Credits Guarantee Department

ECMT
European Conference of Ministers of Transport

EC Relay Centres
Centres to help organisations participate in EC R&D programmes and to disseminate and encourage the exploitation of the results

ED
Employment Department

Education Business Partnerships
See box on page 45

EEA
European Economic Area - a free trade zone covering the countries of the EC, Sweden, Norway, Austria, Finland and Iceland

EEF
Engineering Employers' Federation

EFTA
European Free Trade Area - a grouping composed of Austria, Finland, Iceland, Liechtenstein, Norway, Sweden and Switzerland

Enterprise Networks
Scottish Enterprise, Highlands and Islands Enterprise and their networks of lecs

ERDF
European Regional Development Fund - an EC Structural Fund which co-finances activities such as infrastructure investment and business support measures

EURATOM

European Atomic Energy Community

Eurostat

Statistical Office of the European Communities

FCO

Foreign and Commonwealth Office

FE

Further Education (provided mainly by FE, sixth form and some specialist colleges)

FEFC

Further Education Funding Council

G7

Canada, France, Germany, Italy, Japan, the UK and the United States

GATT

General Agreement on Tariffs and Trade

GCE

General Certificate of Education

GCSE

General Certificate of Secondary Education

GDP

Gross Domestic Product - the total value of goods and services produced during a period of time

Germany

Unless stated otherwise figures in the charts for Germany refer to the territory of the Federal Republic before October 1990

GM

Grant Maintained - the status of schools that have chosen to opt out of local authority control

GNVQ

General National Vocational Qualification (see box below)

Government Regional Offices

Established in April 1994 to bring together the regional operations of DoE, DTp, DTI and the Training Enterprise and Education Directorate of ED

GSVQ

General Scottish Vocational Qualification (see box below)

HE

Higher Education (provided by universities and in some FE colleges)

HEFCs

Higher Education Funding Councils

HMIP

Her Majesty's Inspectorate of Pollution

HSC

Health and Safety Commission

IBB

Invest in Britain Bureau

IEA

International Energy Authority

IMF

International Monetary Fund

Investors in People

The national quality standard for investment in training and development to achieve business goals

ITOs

Industry Training Organisations - sectoral industrial bodies that set training strategy

lecs

Local Enterprise Companies in Scotland which combine business development and training responsibilities and have some functions in common with TECs in England and Wales

MAFF

Ministry of Agriculture Fisheries and Food

Managing in the '90s

DTI initiative offering businesses information and advice on key areas of best management practice

MCI

Management Charter Initiative - an employer-led organisation which promotes the development of managers and has lead responsibility for developing national standards of performance for managers and supervisors within the NVQ framework

MITI
Ministry of International Trade and Industry, Japan

MOD
Ministry of Defence

NACETT
National Advisory Council for Education and Training Targets

National Curriculum
The framework for teaching and learning across a range of subjects and the associated assessment arrangements, laid down in Statute for all pupils of compulsory school age (5-16) attending state schools

NCVQ
National Council for Vocational Qualifications

NICs
National Insurance Contributions

NVQ
National Vocational Qualification (see box below)

OECD
Organisation for Economic Cooperation and Development (for list of members see Chart 1.10 on page 14)

OFSTED
Office for Standards in Education

OST
Office of Science and Technology

OTS
Overseas Trade Services - the Government's export promotion operation

PFI
Private Finance Initiative – see box on page 17

PPP
Purchasing Power Parity - modified exchange rates which adjust for differences in price levels between countries

Privatisation
See boxes on pages 16 and 114

RDOs
Regional Development Organisations - local authority and private sector partnership bodies that promote inward investment in the English regions

RPI
Retail Prices Index

RSA
Regional Selective Assistance - an assistance scheme operated under Section 7 of the Industrial Development Act 1982

RTOs
Research and Technology Organisations - private companies that provide research and associated services on behalf of particular groups of companies which use similar technologies or are in the same sector

S&T
Science and Technology

SCAA
School Curriculum and Assessment Authority

SCE
Scottish Certificate of Education

SFLGS
Small Firms Loan Guarantee Scheme - see para 9.16

Single Regeneration Budget
A fund of public money used to encourage local partners to work together to regenerate local areas in England

SME
Small and medium sized enterprise

Structural Funds
EC Funds which make grants to a range of economic regeneration measures and projects particularly in specially designated areas

SVQ
Scottish Vocational Qualification (see box below)

TCS
Teaching Company Scheme - places high quality recent graduates with companies to carry out supervised projects to encourage technology transfer

Technology Colleges

GM or voluntary-aided secondary schools placing a special emphasis within the National Curriculum on technology, science and maths

TECs

Training and Enterprise Councils - industry-led bodies that set local strategies for training and economic development in England and Wales

TENs

Trans-European Networks - a range of transport, energy and telecoms networks in the EC which may be financed by EC grants, European Investment Bank loans and private sector finance

TVEI

Technical and Vocational Education Initiative - see paras 4.19 and 4.48

UK Unemployment Rate

Rates prior to 1971 are based on the unadjusted number of registrants expressed as a proportion of employees (the unemployed and employees in employment). Rates from 1971 onwards are based on the consistent seasonally adjusted series which expresses the number of unemployed claimants as a proportion of the workforce

UNECE

United Nations Economic Commission for Europe

WTO

World Trade Organisation - the vehicle for implementation of the results of the Uruguay Round of trade negotiations

YT

Youth Training - Government-sponsored work-based training available for all 16 and 17 year old school leavers

VOCATIONAL QUALIFICATIONS AND THEIR EQUIVALENTS

APPROXIMATE DESCRIPTION IN EMPLOYERS TERMS	VOCATIONAL QUALIFICATIONS		ACADEMIC QUALIFICATIONS
	NVQ/SVQ	GNVQ/GSVQ	
Professional Qualifications/ Middle Managers	5	-	Higher Education
Higher Technician/ Junior Manager	4	-	
Technician	3	Advanced	2 A Levels or 3 Highers
Craftsman	2	Intermediate	5 GCSEs (A-C) or SCE Standard Grades
Pre-vocational	1	Foundation	4 GCSEs (D-G) - no equivalent in Scotland

Printed in the United Kingdom for HMSO.
Dd.5062743, 6/94, C3, 51-4225, 5673, 292527.

**This book is to be returned on or before
the last date stamped below.**

19. FEB. 1996
11. MAR. 1996

28. MAR. 1996

25 NOV 1996

11. FEB. 1997

10. MAR 1997

26. JUL 1997

**KENT COLLEGE FOR THE CAREERS SERVICE
HEXTABLE, KENT**

LIBREX